Living Wisdom

Principles for a Life Well Lived

REV. CHAD C. FERNALD

Living Wisdom: Principles for a Life Well Lived

Copyright ©2015 by Rev. Chad C. Fernald

Cover photo © Chad C. Fernald

You may learn more about the author at
www.comfaithnet.blogspot.com

The author may be contacted directly at
comfaithnet@gmail.com

Unless otherwise indicated, all Scripture quotations are from the ESV® Bible (The Holy Bible, English Standard Version®), copyright ©2001 by Crossway, a publishing ministry of Good News Publishers. Used by permission. All rights reserved.

Due to the dynamic character of the internet, web addresses cited in this book may have changed since publication. The author assumes no responsibility for such changes.

Published by Richter Publishing LLC
www.richterpublishing.com

Formatted by: Monica San Nicolas & Diana Fisler

ISBN:0692602542
ISBN-13:9780692602546

DISCLAIMER

This book is designed to provide information on Living Well only. This information is provided and sold with the knowledge that the publisher and author do not offer any legal or medical advice. In the case of a need for any such expertise consult with the appropriate professional. This book does not contain all information available on the subject. This book has not been created to be specific to any individual people or organizations' situation or needs. Reasonable efforts have been made to make this book as accurate as possible. However, there may be typographical and or content errors. Therefore, this book should serve only as a general guide and not as the ultimate source of subject information. This book contains information that might be dated or erroneous and is intended only to educate and entertain. The author and publisher shall have no liability or responsibility to any person or entity regarding any loss or damage incurred, or alleged to have incurred, directly or indirectly, by the information contained in this book or as a result of anyone acting or failing to act upon the information in this book. You hereby agree never to sue and to hold the author and publisher harmless from any and all claims arising out of the information contained in this book. You hereby agree to be bound by this disclaimer, covenant not to sue and release. You may return this book within the guarantee time period for a full refund. In the interest of full disclosure, this book

"Wisdom is the right use of knowledge. To know is not to be wise. Many men know a great deal, and are all the greater fools for it. There is no fool so great a fool as a knowing fool. But to know how to use knowledge is to have wisdom."

~Charles Haddon Spurgeon~

CONTENTS

ACKNOWLEDGEMENTS

The author wishes to express thanks to the following:

~Dr. David C. Alves for his insights into the publishing process

~Ed Marquardt & Rev. Brad Rigney for proof-reading the drafts and for their insights and advice

~The congregations I have been privileged to serve, which have each added something special to my journey: The Church at Spruce Creek (Kittery, ME); Exeter Area Christian Fellowship (Newfields, NH); Hope Community Church (Dover, NH); Community Faith Network (Trinity, FL)

~Jeff & Connie Lander and Corey & Sarah Sesin for financial support

My heartfelt gratitude to these special financial partners without whom this book would not have been possible:

~Keystone Community Church, Lutz, FL~

~"2 Pats Fans"~

~Todd Fernald~

~Kenneth & Sharon Fernald~

~My daughters, through whom I recognize that my pursuit of wisdom is far from over.

~My wife Joleen, my strongest supporter and most faithful friend who has encouraged me every step of the way.

And to my Lord, Who has given me something to say.

INTRODUCTION

Thank you for picking up this book. Whatever your reasons, I trust the Lord Himself has had a guiding hand and intends for you to learn something profitable for your spiritual growth.

The phrase 'Living Wisdom' holds for me a triple meaning. It speaks first to the fact that the wisdom from the Lord is alive and vibrant. In contrast to the writings of the long dead, the Word of God is, as the author of Hebrews tells us, "living and active" (Hebrews 4:12). Secondly, it is a reminder that the wisdom of the Word of God enables us to live balanced and healthy lives; it is wisdom for our daily living. Finally it is a call to walk in the ways of the Lord; to be living out His Wisdom.

I have noticed that in many ways God's people are not ordering their lives, homes or churches on the wise and healthy principles given by the Lord; nor have I come across many resources which attempt to lay out a pattern for ordered, principle based living. My attempt in these pages is to at least begin to offer such a guide for walking and living wisely that I may help people become stronger, healthier, more effective disciples of Jesus Christ.

The Biblical books of wisdom (Job through the Song of Solomon) are a life education manual for God's people. Our focus here is God's Living

Wisdom as it is reflected and revealed primarily, but not exclusively, in the book of Proverbs. Much attention is given to the extended discourse of Proverbs 1:8-9:18 which emphasize the value of heeding wise counsel on some critically important matters. I sense that this discourse is placed at the beginning of the book with the thought that if the reader refuses to heed this early advice, they will not be able to fully appreciate the sayings which will follow. Application of the individual proverbs devoid of a framework of pursuing a whole life pattern of wisdom inevitably becomes a selective process based on one's own feelings rather than on the broader, objective perspective of God's best for His people.

My arrangement is thematic, according to what I see as some of the major topics within Proverbs; those which guide us into God's Wisdom for a life well lived.

I have chosen to use the English Standard Version as the primary English translation in this book and unless otherwise noted, this is to be the assumed version being referenced. The ESV, like many English translations, does not capitalize the pronouns associated with the Godhead. Due to copyrights, I have left these as printed by the ESV, as with other direct quotations, but have capitalized those pronouns in non quoted material.

Throughout the book I will be considering larger portions of Scripture, but due to limits on space I have not included the actual text. Regardless of what version you prefer, it is important that you have your Bible open as you read this book.

Where you see reference to a chapter & verse but no book is named know that I am referring specifically to passages in Proverbs: for example a notation of 2:5 is Proverbs chapter 2 verse 5. All other references are noted as book-chapter-verse (e.g. Psalm 25:2).

The reader will notice the use of the term YAHWEH (generally pronounced 'Yah-way') throughout the book. This Name is comprised of the four Hebrew letters y h w h and is represented in the English with the capitalization, LORD.

The Name YAHWEH is used approximately five thousand times in the Hebrew Scriptures as the unique, self-designated identity of the One True God; the Name which sets Him apart from all 'contenders'.

This is the Name by which God entered into the special covenant agreement with Israel at Mt. Sinai[1]. It is the Name by which the first commandment is issued: "I am [YAHWEH] your God, who brought you out of the land of Egypt, out

---

[1] YAHWEH is the unique and covenantal Name which God reveals to Moses in the encounter at the burning bush. God says to Moses, "I appeared to Abraham, Isaac, and Jacob, as God Almighty, but by my name, [YAHWEH], I did not make myself known to them." (Exodus 6:3) While a reading of those patriarchal accounts shows that God was in fact known and 'called upon' as YAHWEH (see Genesis 9:26; 12:8; 15:7; 25:21), Exodus 6:3 informs us that the primary Name God used for covenant blessing to the patriarchs was 'El Shaddai ('God Almighty').

of the house of slavery. You shall have no other gods before me" (Exodus 20:2-3). YAHWEH was to be the single God Whom Israel was to worship, serve and follow because He is the only God. To acknowledge any other is to commit the grievous sin of idolatry.

This Name is the foundation of the great Hebrew confession of faith, the 'Shema' of Deuteronomy 6:4: "Hear, O Israel: [YAHWEH] our God, [YAHWEH] is one." Because He is the God of Israel, the responsibility falls to the people to honor and respect Him as such and to give their unwavering love and loyalty to Him: "You shall love [YAHWEH] your God with all your heart and with all your soul and with all your might." (Deuteronomy 6:5).

It is YAHWEH, the Living and True God, and the honoring of Him, from which Living Wisdom flows. For these reasons I have made a particular choice in utilizing this Divine Name and have inserted the Name [in brackets] where appropriate in Scripture quotations.

Before getting into our study, I must propose two caveats.

The first is that Scripture is given by God for the benefit of His people. The Bible is not a self-help guide or instruction manual for the world. While the Bible, as the inerrant Word of God, can and does lead non-Christians to salvation, its principles cannot be truly lived out by those who have not been transformed by a work of God's Holy Spirit through the New Birth of faith in Jesus Christ.

The second warning is to understand what a proverb is and is not. A proverb *is* a general life principle which, if followed, make possible a well lived life; a proverb is *not* a guarantee or promise. For example, the lazy does not always go hungry and come to ruin; the diligent do not always have enough; the Lord does not always shower abundance on the generous or withhold good from the stingy; men do not always rejoice in the presence of the righteous nor shrink in horror or fear from the wicked; children do not always turn out faithful.

Certainly it is better to be generous, hardworking and 'good', and our firm belief is that *eventually* the Lord will honor and reward such a life, but we cannot lose heart or give up faith if we do not see results immediately, or ever, on this side of Christ's perfect Kingdom. Proverbs shows us how to live in a healthy, balanced way, but always points us to hope in a relationship with the Lord apart from earthy and temporal results.

Recognizing these matters will keep us from many errors of interpretation. Now let's begin our journey towards discovering Living Wisdom.

Chapter 1

THE NEED FOR LIVING
WISDOM

Have you ever watched a dog chase its tail; or seen a cat furiously pounce after a spot of moving light. Do you ever feel that is what life resembles — something frantic, disjointed and devoid of a coherent framework; in a hurry to go...nowhere?

Early in 2015 a big topic of debate on social media was the color of a dress; was it white and gold, blue and black or some other color? Jonathan Hunt, in an opinion piece on the Fox News website asked,

> "What has happened to us? What has happened to debating the great issues of the day? New ideas on tackling terrorism,

reaching across religious and cultural divides, discussing ways to end poverty in America and around the world, guarding our privacy in the digital era?"[2]

The issue of the dress strikes me as symptomatic of a greater problem of aimlessness in life. People latch on to anything in a search for cohesiveness, even if just for a moment, because they don't know where life is going, how to get there or who to go with.

As reflected by Hunt's op-ed, we major on minor issues and ignore major issues altogether. We no longer know how to rationally dialogue with those who disagree with us, choosing instead to win arguments by shouting the loudest and drowning out the opposing voice. We work too many hours and sleep too few; eat too much and exercise too little; spend beyond our means and are generally dissatisfied with life. Our families are in conflict, our government is adrift and our economy is upside down. The list goes on, but in short, we seem to lack a framework in which life can be well lived.

In this type of world, you would think that those called by the name 'Christian' would have some answers, yet it seems so often the Church is beset with the same problems. Is there an answer?

The Word of God provides the framework we

---

[2] Hunt, Jonathan. *The Internet Gone Mad: Stop talking about white and gold dress. Now.* February 27, 2015. Web. Accessed February 28, 2015

seek; and included in His Word is a special set of books which show us the path to a healthy well lived life. These books include Job, Psalms, Proverbs, Ecclesiastes and the Song of Solomon and are referred to collectively as 'wisdom literature'.

The books of wisdom aid us in understanding and relating to the world around us, connecting us to the human experience. Wisdom draws us all in as real human beings; as equals, not as sub-categories such as man or woman, rich or poor, etc.

The book of Job connects us with the reality of suffering. The Psalms teach us to express joy, sorrow, anger and fear in the framework of faith. Song of Solomon guides us in the appreciation of human love and sexuality. Ecclesiastes stands by our side as we wrestle with the meaning of life.

Proverbs, written mainly by King Solomon, allows us to connect with an even wider array of human experiences, for we all face joy, sorrow, anger, greed, lust and pain. Proverbs is an intensely practical book which, "even without the benefits of modern psychology [understands] the basic human drives and emotions"[3]. There is no type of person who will not find wisdom for living in the practical and challenging insight of the Proverbs. All of us engage in some form of business, such as buying, selling or working. We are all connected to others by some form of relationship. We all live in some form of

---

[3] Merrill, Eugene H. *Kingdom of Priests*. Baker Books: Grand Rapids MI, 2006. Print. p313

community. Regardless of preference of style, everyone has some aesthetic sense and is attracted to some type of artistic expression. The young or old, those just starting out in life or seasoned by the years; the schooled or 'ignorant'; employer, employee or unemployed; parent or child, husband or wife, ruler or subject—and many more, are all laid bare by Proverbs.

Although written over three thousand years ago the wisdom literature, and the principles it contains, remain as relevant as ever. The changing and challenging times we live in certainly require no less wisdom than the days of Job, David or Solomon. Perhaps they require more.

Wisdom literature forces us to face up to the messiness of life and the questions that cannot be answered with clichés and platitudes. Proverbs, like all Biblical wisdom literature, "…summons us to think hard as well as humbly; to keep our eyes open, to use our conscience and our common sense, and not to shirk the most disturbing questions."[4]

Christian singer Natalie Grant wrestles with the messiness of life and the insufficiency of packaged answers in the song *Held*. She sings: "Two months is too little; They let him go; They had no sudden healing. To think that providence would take a child from his mother while she prays is appalling."[5]

---

[4] Kidner, Derek. *The Wisdom of Proverbs, Job & Ecclesiastes*. Intervarsity Press: Downers Grove, IL, 1985. Print. p11
[5] Grant, Natalie. 'Held'. *Awaken*. Digital. Curb. 2005.

Christa Wells, the songwriter, explains these words emerging from a friend's tragic and unexpected loss of their infant son[6]. I wonder, in those dark moments, if well-meaning but poorly informed friends came alongside and tried to offer consolation with the thought that 'God's will' was at work[7].

Because the wisdom literature reflects this messy life, at times it appears to contain contradictory statements. For example, "Answer not a fool according to his folly, lest you be like him yourself" (26:4) seems to be the complete opposite of: "Answer a fool according to his folly, lest he be wise in his own eyes" (26:5).

The first proverb warns us to not stoop to the level of the fool (a type of person we will identify later), to debate him as if he were sensible. The second proverb tells us that a response to the fool is necessary to expose him for who he is, lest he believe he has said something worthwhile or has greater intelligence[8]. Rather than seeing these as competing and contradicting statements, let us look at them as the ends of a single idea: the wise know

---

www.azlyrics.com

[6] Wells, Christa. *What it Means to be Held.* 10/15/2008. Web. Accessed 4/16/2015.

[7] I do believe in God's will and know that there is nothing which takes Him by surprise, but urge caution in expressing poorly considered theological views in times of grief.

[8] Spence H. D. M. & Exell Joseph S. (Editors). *The Pulpit Commentary.* Funk & Wagnalls Co., New York, 1880-1919. Electronic Database: Biblesoft, Inc., 2001.

how to expose fools by turning their own words back on them. Finding this middle, the key idea, leads to a wise life.

There is an implied truth in the books of wisdom; statements of reality which are not up for debate. They tell us, 'this is how the world operates', and our level of comfort with that truth is, respectfully, irrelevant.

A life built on the Living Wisdom of the Bible is a healthy and balanced life. To misunderstand the wisdom tradition is to take a step towards a chaotic life in which no one knows either the reasons things happen or how to affect positive change.

According to 2 Timothy 3:16-17:

> "All Scripture is breathed out by God and profitable for teaching, for reproof, for correction, and for training in righteousness, that the man of God may be competent, equipped for every good work."

The books of wisdom are given for such purpose; they challenge us, command us, confront us with our weaknesses and tendencies to sin and call us to walk a higher and better path befitting the people of God.

~Why Proverbs?

Our study focuses in on wisdom as reflected primarily in Proverbs. A proverb "is a brief, provocative saying that expresses practical wisdom in colorful language. Often it is a principle dressed up as an illustration"[9].

God has given His people the book of Proverbs as a tool through which we may attain Living Wisdom. This is explained in Proverbs 1:2-6. Let's explore these verses.

~*To Know:* Proverbs is written that the reader may "know wisdom and instruction" (1:2a).

The main Hebrew word for wisdom is *hokma* a verb meaning 'to be wise' and which,

> "...represents a manner of thinking and attitude concerning life's experiences; including matters of general interest and basic morality. These concerns relate to prudence in secular affairs, skills in the arts, moral sensitivity, and experience in the ways of the Lord."[10]

Wisdom is not just acting in the right ways; it is thinking the right thoughts, believing in the right things. This internal wisdom then should not fail to manifest itself in life practices, choices, habits and so forth.

Although many ancient cultures had wisdom traditions, the wisdom reflected in the Hebrew literature emphasizes that,

---

[9] Sper, David (Editor). *Knowing God Through Proverbs.* Radio Bible Class, Grand Rapids MI, 1993. Print. p3

[10] Harris, R. Laird, Archer, Gleason L. & Waltke, Bruce K. *Theological Wordbook of the Old Testament.* The Moody Bible Institute of Chicago, 1980 2 Vols. Print. Vol. 1 p282

> "…human will, in the realm of practical matters, was to be subject to divine causes. Therefore, Hebrew wisdom was not theoretical and speculative. It was practical, based on revealed principles of right and wrong, to be lived out in daily life."[11]

The emphasis of the Hebrew wisdom tradition was not a matter of philosophy or academia, but was to encompass all areas of everyday life: parenting, marriage, in the marketplace, on the job, in the bedroom. No activity of life was to be devoid of wisdom's influence.

The word used for instruction (*musar*) does not mean simply the instruction which comes from teaching, but the beneficial moral lessons learned through discipline. Proverbs brings us face to face with our own sins and failures and after boxing us on the ears embraces us and sets our feet on the path to greater moral awareness and ability.

While our human tendency is to recoil from discipline, the Scripture encourages us to accept the remedial work of God in our lives. Job 5:17 affirms this Biblical truth: "Behold, blessed is the one whom God reproves; therefore despise not the discipline (*musar*) of the Almighty." This type of instruction:

> "…teaches how to live correctly in the fear of the Lord…the receptivity for

---

[11] Ibid

'instruction' from one's parents, teacher, [etc] is directly corollary to one's subjugation to God's discipline."[12]

The wisdom literature is a tutor, to borrow and adapt from the Apostle Paul's comments in Galatians 3:24, leading us to seek and to know the Lord. While Paul spoke of the Law as a tutor towards salvation, I suppose we can see Proverbs as a tutor leading us towards a whole and healthy life well lived under the rule of God. If we refuse to heed true wisdom passed on by those with human authority over us, what makes us think we are ready for, or even would desire, God's authority?

God corrects us out of His love with the purpose of equipping us to stay out of future trouble. If we read and receive Proverbs correctly we will 'learn our lessons' before we actually face the trial. As is wisely said, to be forewarned is to be forearmed. Having the information ahead of time can enable us to successfully stand when those particular challenges come upon us.

~*To Understand:* Proverbs is written that one may "understand words of insight" (1:2b).

What passes for understanding in our time? Is it simple comprehension or is there a deeper grasp of a concept which is in mind? The idea in this verse is the latter. The Hebrew verb used in this passage

---

[12] Vine, W.E. *Vine's Expository Dictionary of Biblical Words*. Thomas Nelson Publishers, 1985. Electronic Database: Biblesoft, Inc., 2001

"...refers to knowledge which is superior to the mere gathering of data. It is necessary to know how to use knowledge one possesses."[13]

Proverbs is a living workbook, given that one may learn how to analyze and comprehend God's wisdom. The sayings within proverbs are to be wrestled with, handled and examined closely. They allow us to enter into deep and meaningful discussions about life and truth enabling us to perceive the truth, make that truth a part of our core and then put wise sayings to appropriate use.

~*To Receive:* Proverbs is written that the reader may "receive instruction in wise dealing, in righteousness, justice, and equity" (1:3).

The truest sense of wisdom is not attained by human means, but is given by the Lord, a point we will give greater consideration to in the next chapter. Again the word *musar*, God's corrective, disciplinary care, is used. We stretch out our hand to receive God's gift of curative wisdom with thankfulness and gladness, and as we receive we are enabled to develop in areas which benefit not only our inward growth, but our outward dealings in the world around us.

The gift of wisdom allows us to engage in 'wise dealing' or, in more ordinary terms, common sense. The term used by Solomon "relates to an intelligent knowledge of the reason"[14]. How many times did you need to touch a hot stove before you put two

---

[13] Harris, Archer, and Waltke. p103
[14] Ibid p877

and two together and gained a practical understanding that the hot stovetop causes pain? Armed with that knowledge of cause and effect you use common sense to tell yourself that any hot surface or object is likely to burn; you don't need to touch everything to figure it out again and again. We employ the common sense of Proverbs in matters much more significant.

The gift of wisdom guides us in righteousness. Righteousness is that condition of acting in accordance with the character and nature of God; to be altogether right and just. As fallen creatures, it is impossible that we could ever be perfectly righteous for David says, "no one living is righteous" before God (Psalm 143:2). Solomon is not saying that wisdom *makes* us right before God, but rather, that in receiving and following the principles of Living Wisdom, we are able to discern what is right and true and, like Solomon, we need the help of the Lord to put those principles into practice.

The gift of wisdom sharpens our sense of justice. The Old Testament reveals God's heart for the oppressed and the downtrodden; the Law and the Prophets frequently call God's people to stand for justice in our communities. We must make an important distinction between 'just' and 'fair'. Fairness is a human term in which all sides of a dispute must be treated equally. Justice (Hebrew *tzadiq*) is a divine expression of a verdict which is right and true, even if one party seems to gain over the other.

An example from Solomon's life is the rather well known account in 1 Kings 3 of two women who disputed over which was the actual mother of an infant. Solomon decided to settle the matter 'fairly' by cutting the child in half and giving each woman equal portion. The true mother was willing to renounce her claim to spare the life of the child; the other was willing to let the child die. Solomon returned the child to the true mother. By using wisdom, Solomon was able to achieve 'justice' even though one party went away empty handed. We see so many examples of our culture bowing to the 'tyranny of the fair' while justice is set aside.

The gift of wisdom shows us how to deal in equity. Equity may lead us to think in terms of 'fairness', acting in ways in which all people come out equal. This is not the connotation of the word *yashar*. This word, while not synonymous with *tzadiq* bears some similarities and can be rendered 'uprightness'. Equity "implies the existence and knowledge of the law of God"[15] and indicates that this divine law, or covenant, is being kept. In the cases of the 'good kings' of Judah, it is said that they "*did what was right* in the eyes of [YAHWEH]" (1 Kings 15:11 e.g.); that they were upright in their relationship to God and His Covenant. For one who knows the laws, commands and principles of the Lord, wisdom enables that person also to 'do

---

[15] Ibid p417

right' before the Lord.

Stan Gaede, Provost of Gordon College in the 1990's in a book entitled, *When Tolerance is No Virtue*, relates a personal experience from time spent at UC Berkley. One day he encountered a street evangelist engaged in proclaiming the Gospel. What made the greater impression on Gaede was the voice of opposition from across the street:

> "What struck me...was not the fact of his antagonism but the content. For instead of accusing the evangelist of false teaching, he accused him of false practice; instead of 'Not true, not true,' the chosen mantra of this accuser was 'Unfair, unfair.' What galled him...wasn't the fact that the evangelist proclaimed good news but that he had the audacity to proclaim bad news as well: the very bad news that sinners stand condemned by their sins and need to repent. That was unprincipled. That was unfair. That was intolerance, pure and simple, and it didn't even deserve a hearing."[16]

The man across the street was angry that the message of the evangelist didn't measure up to his standards of 'fairness'. The evangelist was demonstrating 'equity', doing right in the eyes of

---

[16] Gaede, Stan. *When Tolerance is No Virtue*. Intervarsity Press: Downers Grove, 1993. Print. p12

the Lord, but through the eyes of men, was intolerably unfair. Living Wisdom teaches us how to discern the way of God and then how to walk in that way.

~*To Give:* Proverbs is written "to give prudence to the simple, knowledge and discretion to the youth" (1:4).

Prudence is that quality of having good sense and giving careful consideration to our actions. It is taking one's time and not rushing into things. How many times have you done or said something and then immediately wished that time travel was a reality so you could go back and stop yourself? Prudence is that forethought that allows us to avoid the situation in the first place. In more modern idioms, it is 'looking before you leap' or 'thinking before you speak'.

Who are the 'simple' that require such skill? One word study guide identifies such a person as one who may be easily seduced into sinful behavior[17]. Anyone of us might be counted among the simple, for each of us have weak points, places where we are susceptible to being led away from the good path.

Proverbs allows us to see the results of choices before we make them. We do not need to go out and over consume alcohol to learn the hard lessons which Proverbs 23:29-35 teaches us. We do not

---

[17] Biblesoft Inc. and International Bible Translators, Inc. *Biblesoft's New Exhaustive Strong's Numbers and Concordance with Expanded Greek-Hebrew Dictionary.* Electronic Database: Biblesoft, Inc., 1994, 2003, 2006

need to become embroiled in extra-marital affairs to discover the unavoidable disaster which we can find in Proverbs 5, 6 & 7. We all do well to approach Proverbs as the 'simple', knowing our weaknesses and tendencies toward sin. These are the areas the enemy knows to strike because that is where he finds success. To be 'simple' is not necessarily negative, if we recognize our need.

In addition to prudence, Living Wisdom gives "knowledge and discretion to the youth". We know how rash younger people can be; 'full of spit and vinegar' so to speak. Those reading who may be more seasoned in life can certainly recall instances of that impetuous nature. Early in my ministry, I was planning something for our youth group which I did not think all the way through. Thankfully there were some men of 'knowledge and discretion' who came alongside me to say 'no, you won't do that!'

As much as they would like to argue to the contrary, young people do not know it all; they do not have all the answers. Many haven't even figured out which questions to ask! Older folks, weren't you the same? The young are in need of knowledge, not book learning or information overload, but practical, hands on, how-it-really-works, experiential, able to tell good from bad, right from wrong understanding.

This need for practical experience was brought

home to me in something my friend Joe[18] told me. Joe makes his living as a master handyman; he can fix *most* anything (I can't make it seem like he's perfect; I'd never hear the end of it!). The greater part of what he knows he learned from actually doing. He told me once that he was called in on a job that a younger tech had been unable to fix. After a few moments, he was able to identify and remedy the problem. The younger man asked Joe why he was able to succeed. His response was, "I listened". The young tech had been trying to do everything by the book; what he learned in school. Joe applied years of experience which books can't teach, and 'heard' the problem. That's the type of knowledge Proverbs offers.

The verse might move our thoughts only to those who are young in age, and this is the predominant meaning of the word used here (na'ar); yet the word can also carry a nuance of those who might be lacking experience, regardless of age:

> "Jeremiah, while claiming to be only a 'youth,' was not necessarily a youngster. In truth, he argued that he did not have the experience of the older men (Jeremiah 1:6)...Absalom was considered a na'ar, even though he was old enough to lead the troops in rebellion against David (2

---

[18] Name used with permission

Samuel 18:5)."[19]

If the older among us still want to try and wriggle off the hook, see how Proverbs 1 continues: "Let the wise hear and increase in learning, and the one who understands obtain guidance, to understand a proverb and a saying, the words of the wise and their riddles" (1:5-6).

Here is a dose of humility for the more seasoned. No one is ever so smart or wise that they cannot learn more. If you think you are mature in these matters, that's great, but God's word says that you still have a lot to learn!

~Practical Wisdom for Living

What does wisdom do for us as we pursue it? This section of Proverbs helps us to think on the need for Living Wisdom to order and balance our lives.

Solomon urges his son to keep focused on preserving and guarding wisdom as a path to a well lived life: "My son, do not lose sight of these — keep sound wisdom and discretion, and they will be life for your soul and adornment for your neck" (3:21-22). Forgetting the big life lessons is the first step towards disaster. Remembering what we have learned will lead us well.

Wisdom enables the faithful to walk with confidence, trusting that the decisions they make

---

[19] Vine, Electronic Database.

are good and right; this is the purpose of the metaphor in verse 23: "Then you will walk on your way securely, and your foot will not stumble." The one who trusts the Lord and pursues His Living Wisdom is confident to walk with a solid footing, not slipping from the path of goodness to fall into sinful and wicked ways.

Wisdom allows the man or woman of God to correctly understand the world and its evils; to process such things and to remain stable in the face of them, even if evil should touch them, for the wise place their hope in the One Who can deliver.

> "If you lie down, you will not be afraid; when you lie down, your sleep will be sweet. Do not be afraid of sudden terror or of the ruin of the wicked, when it comes, for [YAHWEH] will be your confidence and will keep your foot from being caught" (3:24-26).

Again, please remember, that this is a general principle, not a guarantee in every situation. Our perception is that God sometimes allows evil to overtake His people. This is not a failure on God's part to save His faithful ones; we must accept that His greater plans which we are not privy to are being worked out, and that He will stand with us through any trial. Our confidence comes in knowing that even if evil should be allowed to have its way, a final, perfect deliverance is prepared for a yet future time.

While this is a real hope and truth, it can seem for many to be merely conceptual, lacking practical force for life now. The remainder of our study has as its goal a demonstration of Living Wisdom which impacts us in the 'now'; the present moments in which we live.

*

Have you met yourself here? Perhaps you have come to a point at which you paused and thought, 'I sure could use a bit more Living Wisdom in my life'; 'I'd like to live more confidently'; 'I'd like to be more discerning'. This affirms the reality that we need Proverbs and the wisdom it offers. We want to live well and avoid the disorder in our lives. The wisdom of Proverbs offers God's principles for finding, restoring and maintaining order.

Now that we recognize our need for Living Wisdom, we can move on to consider where this gift may be found.

Chapter 2

THE SOURCE OF LIVING WISDOM

The Wisdom from God's Word is essential if we are to develop a framework for living well before the Lord; but where do we turn to discover this life changing wisdom? It cannot be purchased, for it is without price. It is not found in philosophy, for its principles cannot be reduced to theory. It is not found in books or schools, for even the most unread and unlearned person may grasp wisdom's pearl. Ironically, Solomon himself later writes that "excessive devotion [to books] is wearying to the body" (Ecclesiastes 12:12 NASU).

Wisdom's sole source is YAHWEH the Living God. One commentator noted,

> "Behind every proverb is the personal God of Israel, the self-existent God of our

creation who loves us and longs for us to live in such a way as to bring honor to ourselves and him."[20]

Recognizing God as the wellspring of wisdom reaches back to the ancient book of Job[21] which speaks of wisdom's divine fountainhead: "With God are wisdom and might; he has counsel and understanding" (Job 12:13).

Job 28 is a magnificent expression of the source of Living Wisdom. Wisdom is not found in the depths of earth or sea (Job 28:9-12, 14); neither is it hidden in the palaces or treasuries of kings (Job 28:13). Wisdom is not to be discovered by any craft, skill or device of man (28:9-12) and it cannot be purchased in the market (Job 28:15-19). Wisdom comes only from God. The chapter poses a deep and abiding question: man goes to great lengths to seek out the treasures of the earth—silver, gold, iron, copper (Job 28:1-2), and precious jewels (Job 28:6, 16, 19), but will he show the same ardor for the pursuit of wisdom, the value of which far surpasses those earthly treasures (Job 28:15-19)?

The words of Proverbs 3:13-15 are similar to those found in Job 28, applying a precious quality to wisdom and understanding.

"Blessed is the one who finds wisdom,

---

[20] Sper p6

[21] Job is likely the earliest of all Scripture written perhaps as early as 2000BC. The book reflects a culture which fits the time of the Hebrew Patriarchs Abraham, Isaac and Jacob.

and the one who gets understanding, for the gain from her is better than gain from silver and her profit better than gold. She is more precious than jewels, and nothing you desire can compare with her." (3:13-15)

Often, in both Testaments, the term 'blessed' carries the suggestion of being 'happy', not in terms of external feelings but of inner peace and contentment. The Hebrew term *esher* appears most often in a context of the one who stands in a right relationship to YAHWEH.

Knowing Truth will bring about one of two sensations. Either a person is brought under conviction because they are not living according to that Truth, or the person experiences a sense of peace and tranquility for the hope and encouragement the Truth brings them. It is this latter sense that Solomon speaks of; and what a feeling it is! The sense of security that comes from knowing Truth, from gaining and living by the principles of wisdom, outdoes even the possession of the most valuable and precious earthly materials. And Solomon would be the one to know. He was not only blessed by God with great wisdom, but also became the wealthiest king of his age (see 1 Kings 3:13). When Solomon placed wisdom and riches side by side, the highest value fell to wisdom.

~Wisdom through 'Fear'

Laying hold of wisdom is not found in merely acknowledging God as the source. True wisdom is realized in honoring and revering, also known as 'fearing', God: "And He said to man, 'Behold, the *fear* of the Lord[22], that is wisdom, and to turn away from evil is understanding'" (Job 28:28 my emphasis). We also note Proverbs 1:7, which discloses "the fear of [YAHWEH] is the beginning of knowledge..."

The Hebrew word *ya're* is the common word in the Old Testament for 'fear', used in five different ways: "1) the emotion of fear, 2) the intellectual anticipation of evil without emphasis upon the emotional reaction, 3) reverence or awe, 4) righteous behavior or piety, and 5) formal religious worship."[23]

The fear of YAHWEH relates to the third and fourth of these categories. To fear the Lord is to stand in utter awe and reverence of His power and majesty; the same fear that overcame Isaiah, upon seeing the great vision of God's holiness (Isaiah 6:1-4). A person properly fears the Lord as they recognize the claim of His holiness on their life and their responsibility to submit to Him.

---

[22] In this passage, 'Lord' is in small letters, a translation of another special Name, 'Adonai' which refers also to the One True God and which may be applied to the Messiah as in Psalm 110:1: "[YAHWEH] said to my [Adonai] 'Sit at my right hand until I make your enemies your footstool.'"

[23] Harris, Archer, and Waltke p399

Derek Kidner reflects on this reverence of YAHWEH as the "first principle"[24] of wisdom. This truth "keeps the shrewdness of Proverbs from slipping into mere self interest"[25] and is "the prerequisite for every right attitude"[26].

Eugene H. Merrill also comments, "One should recognize [that] wisdom...had to do with the ability to live life in a skillful way...possessed only by the individual who knew and feared God."[27]

Solomon must have also learned this truth from his father David who wrote: "Come, O children, listen to me; I will teach you the fear of [YAHWEH]" (Psalm 34:11). David understood what it meant to give all honor to his God: "But I, through the abundance of your steadfast love, will enter your house. I will bow down toward your holy temple in the fear of you" (Psalm 5:7).

To cement this understanding in our minds, Psalm 111:10 declares: "The fear of [YAHWEH] is the beginning of wisdom; all those who practice it have a good understanding."

To fear YAHWEH is to revere Him; to give Him all honor and respect, worship and praise; to pray to Him; to obey His commands; to acknowledge Him as Creator, Master, Ruler, Redeemer.

Living Wisdom is the perfect outworking of truth, so it should not surprise us to find that *God*

---

[24] Kidner p17
[25] Ibid
[26] Ibid p19
[27] Merrill p312

Himself is Wisdom, and utilizes the principles of wisdom to the highest degree.

So it was, with the most artistic use of wisdom that He created the universe. Proverbs 3:19-20 attests to creation coming about not through a random series of chance events but planned and rightly ordered by the intelligence of God[28]: "[YAHWEH] by wisdom founded the earth; by understanding he established the heavens; by his knowledge the deeps broke open, and the clouds drop down the dew."

It was by the exercise of perfect wisdom, knowledge and understanding—the skill and awareness of deity—that God founded the heavens and the earth. Creation displays the fingerprints of a supremely intelligent Being, Who established the world for a purpose.

Solomon was given great insight, more than any other of his generation (perhaps *any* generation), into such things. He was a man who studied the world around him; a naturalist (1 Kings 4:33) as well as a poet and a sage. His study of the natural order led him to recognize that God structured the world through wisdom, not chance. How then can a man not understand that his life can and should

---

[28] It seems to me to be an extremely difficult thing to claim belief in the Bible and yet maintain any acceptance or adherence to the various systems of cosmology and origins preached by modern science. My study on the creation leads me to believe that Genesis 1 follows a very structured sequence which is scientifically valid; however I am not a scientist and I leave the reader to explore this topic more deeply through others more qualified to speak to that matter.

be ordered according to the exercise of that same wisdom which is given by God? What darkness fills his heart and clouds his eyes?

This is what the Apostle Paul commented so eloquently about beginning in Romans 1:18. Echoing Psalm 19, Paul declares that the created order displays the marks of the One God so clearly that a person who rejects Him is "without excuse" (1:20).

> "For although they knew God, they did not honor him as God or give thanks to him, but they became futile in their thinking, and their foolish hearts were darkened. Claiming to be wise, they became fools..." (Romans 1:21-22)

Denial and rejection of God leads a person into a life of deeper and more profound unrighteousness. Scripture calls such person a 'fool'.

~*The Fool*

Man's rejection as identified by Paul in the above quoted passage from Romans, is rooted in the second part of Proverbs 1:7: "fools despise wisdom and instruction." Proverbs uses two main words to describe the 'fool'.

The first is *eviyl*, a type of person who:

> "...generally lacks wisdom; indeed, wisdom is beyond his grasp. In another nuance, 'fool' is a morally undesirable

individual who despises wisdom and discipline. He mocks guilt, and is quarrelsome and licentious. Trying to give him instruction is futile."[29]

This 'fool' is seen as one who is morally deficient; the word being used to refer "primarily to moral perversion or insolence, to what is sinful rather than to mental stupidity."[30]

This type of person cares only for their own gain or good. They are quarrelsome (20:3) and short tempered (12:16) and continually shoot their mouth off (10:14) revealing their true nature. These, says Proverbs 1:7, have utter contempt for the Way and Word of God. They are unreachable and unteachable, believing they have all the answers. The fool figures prominently in certain passages which define the wise life as a life which seeks instruction. The eviyl is boorish, lustful, prideful and morally bankrupt, and, unless the penetrating Spirit of God gets to him or her, they are utterly lost.

Another term used in Proverbs is *nabal*. This manner of fool, like the *eviyl* is morally and spiritually insensitive both of which "close the mind to reason"[31]. This is the type of fool as David wrote, who "says in his heart, 'There is no God.' They are corrupt, they do abominable deeds, there

---

[29] Vine, Electronic Database
[30] Harris, Archer, and Waltke p19
[31] Ibid p547

is none who does good" (Psalm 14:1).

The reader familiar with the life of David will recognize this word, *nabal*, as the name of a very rash and foolish man David encountered in 1 Samuel 25. His servants classed him as "...such a worthless man that one cannot speak to him" (1 Samuel 25:17), and even his own wife, Abigail, defined him as a "worthless fellow, Nabal, for as his name is, so is he. Nabal is his name, and folly is with him" (1 Samuel 25:25).

Was there ever a man so aptly named? Abigail makes a word play on his name as she tells David to take no heed of *Nabal* because he is *unbaalaah* ('folly'). Interestingly in both cases the Hebrew literally reads 'son of belial'. The Hebrew *beliya'al* can mean worthless or is used in places as a name for satan[32]. Thus the man Nabal was a 'son of worthlessness', but worse, a 'son of the devil'. The fool is, in effect, placing himself under the rule of evil and its prince.

The fool is of the same kind as those living in the days of the Judges who "did what was right in his own eyes" (Judges 17:6; 21:25). In those days the corrupt nature of the Israelites was compounded by the lack of a king in Israel. In the case of the fool, they have rejected God as King of their lives. If wisdom begins with knowing and revering YAHWEH, giving Him ultimate honor and respect, worship and praise, it follows as utterly impossible

---

[32] I realize it is technically incorrect, but I personally never capitalize the name of the enemy.

for the fool, if they continue to "despise wisdom and instruction", to attain Living Wisdom.

Pause here to reflect on your life. When are we prone to play the role of the fool? "Oh no!" you say. "I don't despise the Way of the Lord!" Perhaps not to the degree of the Proverbial fool, but aren't there, if we are honest, areas of our lives that we fail to yield to the Kingship of the Lord? Maybe in our finances, where it seems so many Christians feel God's authority does not extend. Perhaps some reading this have bought into the climate of sexual 'liberty' and reject God's lordship over their sexuality.

Whatever it might be, if we have not yielded areas of our life to the Lord, or worse *refuse* to do so, and fail to heed His principles for wise and healthy living we are dangerously close to the life of the fool. If we attempt to excuse and justify our failings the fool in us rises up. If we think we can ignore or neglect the value of Proverbs for all seasons of life we are acting as the fool.

According to the Scripture, to truly 'know' is to act in accordance with that knowledge. Let's say I tell my kids that we will be leaving in 15 minutes for an appointment and they respond, 'I know', but then do not make any move to get ready to go; do they truly 'know'? A demonstration of appropriate behavior, such as using the restroom or putting on their shoes is in order to prove the knowledge is real. An example: "Whoever is righteous has regard for[33] the life of his beast (12:10); accordingly such a person takes care of his animal by feeding and sheltering it. A believer can say that they 'know' what God desires from them, but if they do not demonstrate behavior suitable to that claim, or worse, go out and do the opposite, the Scripture says that they do *not* know. This is more severe than simply making poor choices or being weak; it is about being a fool.

To have Living Wisdom is to follow a life pattern which leads to length of days, prosperity and peace (so see Proverbs 3:16-17). To be a fool closes one off to the benefits which can result from a life well lived before the Lord.

It seems that later in his life Solomon forgot the value of wisdom, expending his energy in pursuit of worldly things. Ecclesiastes, if written by Solomon looking back on his life, seems to capture a return to a right way of thinking and living. He says, "The end of the matter; all has been heard. Fear God and keep his commandments, for this is the whole duty of man" (Ecclesiastes 12:13). In these words Solomon assesses his life and concludes that a life without reverence for God and obedience to His ways is no life at all.

Do we rightly estimate the value of knowing the Lord and His ways, and the value of walking in those ways? Have we pushed the possession of wisdom further down the list than we might care to

---

[33] Literally, 'knows'

admit? I urge you to make the decision to heed the wisdom of Proverbs and to hear the voice of the Lord speaking through His Word, that you might determine in your heart never to allow the fool get the better of you!

~*Wisdom's Living Voice*

What better source can we turn to for Living Wisdom than that which God has provided for us in His Word? In Proverbs 8:22-36, the book seems to take on a life of its own. I will confess that I do not know all the ins and outs of how the Holy Spirit worked to inspire the writers of Scripture; yet I believe it to be true and in this chapter Solomon seems to step back as the Spirit takes the pen. While the words are similar to what has been written previously, there is a different tone.

'Lady Wisdom' herself (more on her later) steps forward to make her case as the good and true path. She declares, "from my lips will come what is right, for my mouth will utter truth...all the words of my mouth are righteous; there is nothing twisted or crooked in them" (8:6-8).

By what right can this personified wisdom make such a claim? What makes this path of wisdom more valid than that of the Egyptians or the Babylonians or the Greeks? The answer lies in the antiquity of this particular wisdom. Egyptian wisdom dates back to 2500BC; Mesopotamian and Babylonian wisdom is likely as old. Yet these traditions are children compared to Lady Wisdom. She has existed for far, far longer.

> "[YAHWEH] possessed me at the beginning of his work, the first of his acts of old. Ages ago I was set up, at the first, before the beginning of the earth. When there were no depths I was brought forth, when there were no springs abounding with water. Before the mountains had been shaped, before the hills, I was brought forth, before he had made the earth with its fields, or the first of the dust of the world" (8:22-26).

Is this not what was referred to earlier: "[YAHWEH] by wisdom founded the earth" (3:19)? Wisdom, in this context, is not God, but comes from God. Wisdom was created by God, but is not a 'creature' that we could catalog or display in a zoo. More to our specific point, this wisdom is ancient, predating mountains, seas and skies; the very creation itself. Therefore this wisdom predates anything and everything man has conceived in his own mind.

Why does a 1909 Honus Wagner baseball card fetch 2.4 million dollars today when it was barely worth pennies then? What happens to increase the value of a five-cent coin to over twenty dollars? One answer is age. The older something is, the more precious it often becomes, even if when it was 'new' it was cheaply used and discarded. Another factor in the increase of value is scarcity. Rare items such as books which have fallen out of print, that baseball card (less than 60 in the world) or stamps such as the sole existing British Guiana One-Cent stamp are valued because they are so unique.

The wisdom being spoken of in Proverbs 8 is the oldest, preceding the creation itself, and the rarest, unique as it comes not from the thoughts of men but from the mind of God Himself. These two aspects give 'Lady Wisdom' the right to claim the attention and adherence of all people. As a result she can say:

> "And now, O sons, listen to me: blessed are those who keep my ways. Hear instruction and be wise, and do not neglect it. Blessed is the one who listens to me, watching daily at my gates, waiting beside my doors. For whoever finds me finds life and obtains favor from [YAHWEH], but he who fails to find me injures himself; all who hate me love death" (Proverbs 8:32-36).

The rejection of Living Wisdom is a rejection of the source of that wisdom and evidences a love affair with death. This is a claim to absolute truth, a claim which is unpopular in a culture that rejects absolutes; but when examined closely, it is the only claim which is valid for it is God Himself Who speaks. To heed these words is life and blessing, the "favor" (*ratsah*, 'delight') of God.

*

Mankind has explored the depths of the earth and sea and even now beyond the edges of our solar system in the attempt to seek 'truth' and understanding. Comets we are told may contain matter which gives us clues into understanding our origins. New fossils may finally show us the path of our development. Yet almost exclusively these quests omit the 'fear of the Lord'. Like the fool, they not only say in their heart, but proclaim with their mouths that "There is no God" (Psalm 53:1). Religion and things of the spiritual nature, they say, cannot help in the quest for truth; 'science'[34], reason, man's innate sense is what we must trust in our search. "God looks down from heaven on the children of man to see if there are any who understand, who seek after God" (Psalm 53:2) but all have abandoned Him. We have traded the absolute 'thus says YAHWEH' for the ever shifting 'scientists think that'…and then we are surprised at the aimless wandering of modern life.

We declare that the sole source for true, Living Wisdom, is the God Who created all things, Who revealed Himself in acts of history, in the canvas of nature, in the written Scripture and ultimately in

---

[34] These statements are not a rejection of science itself, but a criticism of a humanistic 'pseudo-science' which preaches untested and un-testable theory as fact and tyrannically excludes any position based in the 'the fear of the Lord'.

the person of Jesus of Nazareth. It is only by beginning in humble awe and reverence of this True and Living God that truth and wisdom can be attained. Anything less ends in folly. Which Source Will You Choose?

Be Wise.

Chapter 3

GUIDES TO LIVING WISDOM

As I trust it is your desire to seek God's Living Wisdom on His terms, we now move on to consider those that can guide us in this discovery.

~Better than an After School Special

Those who grew up with pre-cable television looked forward to those times set aside just for children's programs; shows ranging from Howdy Doody to Captain Kangaroo to Bugs Bunny. My formative years were the late 1970's and early 1980's a staple of which were the Saturday morning back-to-back-to-back cartoon lineups. Additionally, I remember a short window of opportunity from about 2:00-5:00pm on weekdays, if there was a clear enough signal to be picked up by the VHF/UHF 'rabbit ears' (who remembers that gadget?). An important component of these programming hours was the myriad of Public Service Announcements, such as *One to Grow On* or *The More You Know*. We were also treated to After School Specials highlighting contemporary issues faced by kids.

Through these means I learned how to pick healthy foods, how to practice good dental habits, how the digestive system worked, how to stand up to bullies and the importance of keeping the pot handles turned in! These provided good information—important and helpful in some respects; but were they the influences I really needed? Did they teach me how to avoid sin, how to work hard, save my money, love my wife, discipline my kids?

No. Those things that really matter require a different type of influence, something of far greater value than an after school special.

~Intergenerational Wisdom

~Father Knows Best

Proverbs 1:8 begins with the words "Hear, my son…" The address 'my son' appears twenty three times in Proverbs, fifteen of those in chapters 1-7. The word 'son' by itself appears an additional twenty one times, mainly as the subject of a proverb.

Some interpreters see this as a general expression of "a teacher's fatherly way of speaking to a pupil"[35]. I do not reject this position, yet I see the book take on deeper meaning if we recognize the address not merely as a literary device, but rather as an intensely personal appeal from Solomon to his own children.

This repeated use of the familial term 'son' also impresses upon me the reality of something wonderful and vital, yet something we have seemingly lost; the importance of intergenerational influence for the passing on of truth and wisdom.

It is the responsibility of each generation to pass on honor for God and His teachings to the next generation, a precedent clearly established in Deuteronomy 6:7:

> "You shall teach [YAHWEH's Word] diligently to your children, and shall talk of them when you sit in your house, and when you walk by the way, and when you lie down, and when you rise."

When a new king came to the throne of Israel, one of his first responsibilities was to sit under the guidance of the priests and write out a personal copy of the Law which he was to keep with him constantly: "and he shall read in it all the days of his life, that he may learn to fear [YAHWEH] his God by keeping all the words of this law and these statutes, and doing them" (Deuteronomy 17:18-19).

---

[35] Kidner p19

Assuming Solomon followed this directive he would have read, copied and pondered the words from Deuteronomy 6 and perhaps this was his motivation for addressing Proverbs to his son.

Writing with imperative Solomon urges his son to learn the wisdom of the ages, to take the lessons to heart; to hear the instructional warnings offered from his father and to not forsake the 'laws' and 'precepts' passed on by his mother (1:8). Proverbs clearly points us to the wisdom of our parents which continues on even after we are grown: "Listen to your father who gave you life, and do not despise your mother when she is old" (23:22).

~The Wisdom of the Ages

Wisdom is nurtured not only through direct parental care and compassion but by extension this intergenerational responsibility includes grandparents, aunts, uncles and other older family members.

Scripture declares Solomon to be the wisest of all men (1 Kings 4:30-34) and this was without question a special gift from God; but in addition to divine gifting Proverbs 4 reveals that Solomon was also the beneficiary of generational wisdom: "When I was a son with my father, tender, the only one in the sight of my mother, he taught me" (4:3-4). As Solomon urges his own sons towards wisdom's path, we receive a glimpse of his own training in the ways of wisdom received at the feet of his own father, King David[36]. The Living Wisdom being expressed is not only father to son, but grandfather to grandson.

'Grandfather' David recognized that life was found in keeping the commandments of God (4:4) and that the pursuit of wisdom was the highest ideal (4:6-9). David knew that he had been taught by YAHWEH and this way of life was the most important teaching he could pass on not only to his son, but to all the generations which would follow.

From ancient times up to the Industrial Revolution and even into the early 20th Century, families lived and grew in close proximity (think of the intergenerational living reflected in such classic television programs as *The Waltons*); if not in the same house then at least on the same street. Today, the rapid advancement of technology seems to have given the impression that the wisdom of the older generation is 'obsolete'. Combine this with our cultural propensity to send our seniors into secluded living, and we have amputated a major resource from our collective body.

I was very close to my paternal grandmother. She was born in August of 1906 and passed away in May of 2004. Think on that span of 97 plus years; consider all that she witnessed in her lifetime. When she was born, Civil War veterans

---

[36] When we think of David's words, we turn to the books of Samuel and the Psalms, so perhaps you never knew that Proverbs also preserves some of his sayings, thoughts and perspectives on Living Wisdom.

were still around to recall their experiences. She remembered horse drawn carriages in downtown Portsmouth, NH and railways as the main means of transportation. By her death, she had witnessed supersonic aircraft, automobiles that could reach speeds of 300 mph and the development of rockets and space shuttles. She remembered the influenza epidemic of 1919. For the first ten years of her life there was no such thing as the Soviet Union; Europe was dominated by the Austrian and German empires. She lived through two World Wars, the conflicts in Korea and Vietnam, the 1991 Gulf War and the events of 9/11. To her, WWI was 'The World War' and WWII was 'The Hitler War'. She saw the 'roaring twenties', the Great Depression and the major social changes from 1940 to 2000. Her life spanned the gramophone to the iPhone; silent films to digital 3-D. How amazed she would have been if she had lived five to ten years more!

My father was born in October of 1939. Veterans of the Spanish American War were in their seventies and WWI was only twenty one years past. He has early recollections of blackout drills during WWII. He remembers taking a train from Portsmouth, NH into Boston, walking up to the ticket window at Fenway Park and getting a good seat for 'pennies'; these days a Sox ticket is among the most expensive in all of professional sports. His heroes of the hometown nine were Ted Williams, Dom DiMaggio and Johnny Pesky. As a young teenager he rooted for Otto Graham and the Cleveland Browns, and Y.A. Tittle and the New York Giants because there were no New England Patriots. He delivered milk door to door. When he was born there was no United Nations or NATO.

I was born in November of 1972. The Vietnam conflict was nearing an end. President Nixon had not yet been implicated in the Watergate affair. I remember 8-Track tapes and rabbit ear antennas. I watched Roger Clemens strike out 20 Seattle Mariners in 1986 on a black and white TV with no cable hookup! For most of my growing up years, my dad was the chief of the volunteer fire department in Greenland, NH. In the mid-late 1970's there was no county dispatcher in southeast NH. In our kitchen was a red phone—I kid you not, a RED PHONE! It was the dedicated fire line because there was no 9-1-1. A direct fire call would come in and my mother would begin alerting the volunteer fire fighters.

My point in all this, and many of you reading surely have similar recollections, is the vast wealth of knowledge and experience accumulated in the generations before us. Solomon calls this wisdom of the generations "a graceful garland for your head and pendants for your neck" (1:9). Just as a gold necklace or diamond earrings can enhance the grace and beauty of a woman, so the wisdom passed on by godly parents and grandparents, when heeded and lived out, will make the life of the listener more beautiful.

Let me state again that true Living Wisdom is found only in those who know and revere God as Lord. We must not assume that simply because one is older they possess wisdom. Proverbs 16:31 says, "gray hair is a crown of glory; it is *gained in a righteous life*" (my emphasis). The honor of a wise life comes from living a righteous life; a life of obedience to and honor for the Lord. It is from those who are counted as righteous on God's terms—faith in His provision of Jesus Christ as Savior and Lord.

What about those who do not have believing parents or grandparents? I would suggest that Proverbs 23:22 could be applied also to those who are counted as spiritual parents; men and women who birthed and reared us in the faith. One who is pursuing a wise life will seek out and give their serious attention to the sage advice of godly men and women, whether natural or spiritual parents. I have men in my life to whom I can turn for spiritual counsel and life wisdom; men who have 'fought the battles' and found God's truth to guide them through.

Living Wisdom calls us to establish relationships with those in our lives who can lead us to greater wisdom, as well as with those to whom we may begin to impart wisdom. There are abundant resources in our congregations, Christian seniors who can no longer be active in the day-to-day life of the Church, who may not even be able to attend scheduled services, but whom, if we would take the time to go to their homes and sit with them, are ready and willing to fill our lives with their lessons.

God has blessed us with the wisdom of the faith community to guide us, to 'deliver' us (28:26), to keep us from the 'way of death' which seems right to us until it is exposed (14:12; 16:25). It brings us blessing and understanding and the 'fountain of life' (13:14).

This interaction of generations within homes stands in stark contrast to the segmentation, or worse the *fragmentation* within local churches, which is doing great damage to the Body of Christ.

In far too many traditional settings (buildings with pews and pulpits) families do not learn, worship or grow *together*. The youngest are sent to the nursery while the oldest drop out of life-long learning. Kids receive teaching the intellectual equivalent of cotton candy while most adults eat 'potato chips' consisting of fill-in-the-blank worksheets devoid of any real need to think critically about Scripture and Faith and how these affect daily life. People are taught *what* to think, not *how* to think, about the important matters of faith. Using platitudes and clichés teachers offer snippets of information and call it 'knowledge', but fail to impart any real wisdom for living.

These words may seem hard, but the results of continuing to follow this path are deadly. These systems succeed in making 'members' of congregations but fail to make *disciples of Jesus*. As a result they produce Christian alcoholics, Christian gamblers, Christian astrologists, Christian pornographers…they make 'fools'.

I followed these patterns because that was how I was trained. I was wrong to do so. God's people must be more deeply engaged in the process of thinking deeply and critically about the Word of Truth and the transmission of wisdom and truth from generation to generation, vital in God's purposes for His people, cannot be replaced by the teaching of a 'professional pastor' one or two hours a week.

Because of these realities impressing themselves upon me, I underwent a radical shift in my philosophy of ministry. I was led away from traditional religious settings in favor of small home based fellowships which reach out to neighbors and families in the intimate surroundings of living room couches and kitchen tables. In these settings, children are an integral part of the teaching-learning process and parents are invited into the center of faith training, being equipped and supported by leaders who have a passion for shepherding believers. I deeply believe this allows us to better uphold the profoundly important mandate for establishing every believer in the Faith, making them into disciples who can be trusted to carry on the Truth to the next generation (see 2 Timothy 2:2).

Can you begin to understand what are we losing in the separation of the generations in our churches? Perhaps it is not something you had ever considered before or perhaps you also have been concerned over this problem. No matter if you are a leader in the local congregation or simply a regular participant; I believe it is critical that you begin to ask the questions of how to recover intentional intergenerational connection and dialogue in the Body of Christ.

~*The Company We Keep*

Just as Living Wisdom teaches us about positive influences, so also it has much to say about the dangers of allowing the wrong influences into our lives.

One of the ways the enemy attacks and weakens believers is through damaging relationships; 'friends' who do not seek the Lord and would lead us away from wisdom: "My son, if sinners entice you do not consent...do not walk in the way with them; hold back your foot from their paths" (1:10, 15).

In Proverbs 1:10-19 it is as if we see Solomon taking his son by the shoulders, looking him straight in the eye and imploring him: 'Son, sin looks good, it sounds fun and it may even seem to pay off, but it is poison. It leads to death. And those who would lead you down those paths—you don't need them in your life.'

I spent a couple years teaching in a local Christian high school. One of my students, we'll call him Ned, was on the fast track to a life of disaster. Bitter and rude, he was barely passing any classes. Every teacher, it seemed, had given up on him. And yet Ned talked often about wanting to enter the ministry. Finally I confronted Ned and told him plainly that unless he changed the path he was on, he had better forget about the ministry. I think it was the first honest conversation about the importance of character anyone had ever had with this young man. Over the next seven months, Ned went through a remarkable transformation as he surrendered to the Lord. His attitude was completely changed, his grades went up, he dropped some unhealthy weight and, to illustrate my point here, he cut off unhealthy 'friendships' that were a drain on his spiritual growth. He and I had daily conversations about faith and life and I am proud to say that he completed studies at a well respected Bible college and entered ministry. Ned knew that there were people who he once considered to be friends, but who, in reality, were poisoning his life. He did the wise thing, a hard thing to be sure, and cut ties.

Perhaps we have childhood friends whose paths of life led away from the Lord, yet we still keep counsel with them. Or perhaps we spend our time in the company of those who lead us into poor habits and choices. If we are not pursuing wisdom rooted in the reverence of the Lord, we will have greater difficulty in choosing friends and companions who benefit us in our faith walk;

influences which entice us rather into sin. The example Solomon presents is extreme: 'friends' who lead others to do unspeakable acts of evil.

The foundation of Solomon's plea is an understanding of sin: "My son, if *sinners* entice you..." The Hebrew word *chata* is a common term for sin ('to miss the mark'). If we are going to pass on wisdom, or learn wisdom for ourselves, we must recover what seems to be a fading, if not lost, understanding of sin.

The Bible assumes that we know what sin is but to be certain, gives us enough information that we may formulate a definition. Sin is anything, action, thought or intent, which violates the Word, Will or Way of God, rightly understood and interpreted.

If we still remain unsure as to what constitutes a 'sinner', we are given a vivid description. These sinners are those who 'entice' us. The Hebrew *pathah* can simply mean 'to persuade', but more often has the more sinister connotation of 'deluding' or causing one to act by deceiving them. These people use clever words which make their ways seem good and right. Think back to Genesis 3 in which we are given a front row seat to witness how satan, the original sinner, planted the rotten seeds which corrupted the first parents. They were deviously enticed. Sinners take what God created for good and twist it to perverse ends.

The culture we live in today tells us to rush into whatever behavior we want and someone else will clean up the mess. We are told to take life easy and let someone else foot the bill. We are told that a lifetime commitment to one spouse is archaic and we should 'play the field'. We are told to let our children make their own choices and not impose boundaries on them.

God's Living Wisdom challenges all these assertions with more than just 'do this' or 'don't do that' or 'because I say so'. Solomon speaks with reason and reasons. Do not go along with sinners because their twisted perspectives will lead you to disaster.

The passage reveals greater detail about the make-up of a 'sinner'. These evil doers "lie in wait for blood" and "ambush the innocent without reason" (1:11). They are psychopaths haunting shadowy alleyways in the dark of night, waiting for unsuspecting passersby to wander too close. They look for "precious goods" (1:13), spoil with which to fill their houses, fattening themselves at the expense of their victims. They snatch purses, break into houses, loot stores, hack bank accounts, steal bitcoins, commit insurance fraud and swindle the elderly out of their savings.

Solomon warns his son:

> "...these men lie in wait for their own blood; they set an ambush for their own lives. Such are the ways of everyone who is greedy for unjust gain; it takes away the life of its possessors" (1:18-19).

They say 'what goes around comes around'.

While as Christians we do not espouse the notion of karma, we do understand that God will bring back onto the sinner the 'reward' of his sin.

Solomon had firsthand experience with this. Soon after the death of his father David, Solomon was faced with three men who had plotted evil; Adonijah, Joab and Shimei. Solomon was God's agent to bring justice to these men (you can read these episodes in 1 Kings 2). So when Solomon writes to his son concerning the fate of the 'sinner', he is not speaking theoretically. He knows that the end of the sinner is certainly blood and death; their own.

We can never completely avoid 'sinners' nor are we supposed to hide away from the world (see 1 Corinthians 5:9-10). The problems arise when we take irreverent, unrepentant people as confidants and counselors. This is a path to our own destruction.

Bad company comes at us not only from the outside, but also from within our own minds. Trusting our own advice, independent of any guidance, especially if we are not thinking clearly on a matter, can also be a recipe for trouble. Proverbs warns us against 'keeping company with ourselves'. We read that "the way of a fool is right in his own eyes" (12:15) and "whoever trusts in his own mind is a fool" (28:26). We are not meant to be islands unto ourselves. This also is a path to ruin.

Proverbs tells us that "a wise son hears his father's instruction, but a scoffer does not listen to rebuke" (13:1). The 'scoffer' is a contemptible individual, "an abomination to men" (24:9) who thumbs his nose at and derides all things good; the "haughty man who acts with arrogant pride" (21:24). He is like the fool who "despises his father's instruction" (15:5). The 'scoffer' sees no value in the wisdom of the generations. He refuses to "listen to advice and accept instruction" that he "may gain wisdom in the future" (19:20). When his life collapses around him, he will not consider the choices that led him to his own ruin, but will vent his anger against man and God. He can never accept that his own wisdom is not sufficient to guide him well.

*

A ministry colleague once told me, 'everyone should have three people in their life: a Paul, a Barnabas and a Timothy.' What he meant was that a person should have a spiritual mentor (a Paul), one who is at about the same place in their faith walk as they are (a Barnabas) and someone in whom to invest and be a mentor to (a Timothy). Wise counsel! I would encourage you to take time and prayerfully consider those spiritually mature people who you might seek out to be your mentors and guides; think also about people at the same place as you with whom you share faith and life and finally who you know that you could become a guide to.

The Living Wisdom to be gained from the older

generations and passed on to the next generation is vital to the continued health of the Church.

Be Wise.

Chapter 4

LIVING WISDOM FROM THE INSIDE OUT

Before Living Wisdom can truly manifest itself in our lives, it must transform us from the inside out. Outwardly we could appear to others as if we are growing in wisdom though inwardly we might be in turmoil. We are embattled by a variety of influences, both internal and external, which combine to unbalance our hearts and minds. This disruption in the way we feel, think and ultimately act hinders the discovery and practice of Living Wisdom.

The Hebrew word commonly used for the 'mind' is *leb* or *lebab*, which more properly translates as 'the heart' and refers to the 'inner man'; the area of our will and desire. The Old

Testament often combines 'heart' (*leb*) and 'soul' (*nephesh*) to emphasize *the whole person* and there is little to show that the Hebrews divided the head and the heart as western thought often does[37]. Therefore, because the whole person is in view, whatever affects one aspect of life necessarily influences the rest. Living Wisdom is the means by which every part of life may be balanced making possible a life well lived.

~Inward Challenges to Developing Wisdom

Character does not begin on the outside but is developed from within us. The convictions we hold, the boundaries we set, our ethical views and so on, develop in that 'leb' center of our being.

Living Wisdom has much to say regarding our general character; such things as our motives, the integrity behind our actions as well as the due rewards for right behavior and the consequences of dealing falsely with others. Living Wisdom helps us identify the right and the wrong types of character traits and teaches us how to choose the good over the evil. While the list is long, I offer just a few more prominent challenges.

---

[37] It is my perspective that to take these statements or others such as 'heart, soul and strength' or in the NT 'body, mind and spirit' as teaching man as a divided being is a mistake and stands outside the Biblical understanding of man as a unity. The Bible knows nothing of 'compartmentalizing' life.

~Arrogant Pride

Of all the character flaws known to man, it could be argued that the supreme issue is pride. Pride looks to depose God in favor of the 'self' as king in the deepest inner place where will and desire are determined. Pride 'lifts up' a heart and causes one to "forget [YAHWEH] your God" (Deuteronomy 8:14). Pride is, when all is said and done, giving in to the temptation of satan to "be as God" (Genesis 3:5).

The Old Testament is replete with evidences of pride leading to the corruption of morality; men of otherwise upstanding character brought low in pride. In this regard, many are familiar with the well known proverb, "pride goes before destruction and a haughty spirit before a fall" (16:18). Solomon's own father, David, a man of great faith and moral fiber, succumbed on two occasions to a prideful spirit (see 2 Samuel 11-12 and 24). In both cases David learned the hard way, as we sometimes must, that pride is a killer. YAHWEH brought judgment which humbled the shepherd-king and cast a shadow across his otherwise righteous reign.

Truly Solomon could write: "When pride comes, then comes disgrace" (11:2) and "before destruction a man's heart is haughty" (18:12). How much better if we would learn that "with the humble is wisdom (11:2) and "humility comes before honor" (18:12). People of great character are people with limits on their pride.

There is a difference between being arrogantly prideful and being proud of an accomplishment or a job well done or even being the thankful recipient of praise. The former places all the glory on ourselves; puffs us up and makes us feel not just self-important, but superior. This type of pride says, 'thank you, it's about time you recognized me for the wonder that I am!' This is also what we call 'hubris'. The other, type of pride genially acknowledges the grace of the Lord or the result of hard work or skill (there are humble people who are not believers). A person is grateful for the recognition, but it does not change their general character. They don't consider themselves better than anyone else. This type of pride says, 'thank you, I appreciate the recognition, now let's move on.'

Because pride puts the self at the center, it leaves no room for the Lord or His ways. Living Wisdom teaches me how to step back and return my focus to the Lord and His work. As the prideful spirit is done away with I set foot on the path of living well before the Lord.

~Hypocrisy

Hypocrisy is an ugly offshoot of pride. If we arrogantly believe we are the law unto ourselves, then we will always choose to act in ways that ultimately benefit ourselves. What looks like charity is in reality a means for a tax write off; what seems like kindness is a mask for self-aggrandizement. This is the type of hypocritical behavior among many of the Pharisees and which was so roundly chastised by Jesus.

If on the other hand we believe that there is a law outside of ourselves and that we are accountable to that law and Law Giver, charity is for the benefit of the other person; kindness is true; giving is done from obedience to God rather than to gain financial benefit.

Solomon wrote that "The righteousness of the blameless keeps his way straight, but the wicked falls by his own wickedness" (11:5). The "righteousness of the blameless" is an inner character quality of truth and goodness; one who is morally and spiritually pure before God. This is not a natural condition for humans corrupted by sin, but is a gift granted to those who have been redeemed through the work of Jesus. The person who possesses such integrity of character lives with confidence and without regret. By contrast the wicked possesses a crooked character and in the end this lack of moral or spiritual fiber will do them in. They may lose a job or a spouse or a friend. They will eventually be led to ruin, if not in this life, then when they stand before their Judge.

Solomon also writes that "the thoughts of the righteous are just" (12:5) and that "a man of crooked heart does not discover good" (17:20). These passages allow us to see that integrity or the lack thereof, is not primarily an outer quality, but an inward character trait. Living Wisdom challenges our motives and places the spotlight on the integrity of our character and how we live that character out.

During the summer of 2015 the adult website 'Ashley Madison'[38] experienced a massive data breach which exposed the personal information of millions of its clients. In the aftermath, several people committed suicide and it can be certain that many other lives and homes were disrupted and even destroyed by this event; proving the proverb true that 'wickedness' led to the fall of many. No one who put themselves out there on that site could have ever truly believed that it wouldn't somehow come back to bite them, could they?

Someone commented on a radio program how the 'self-righteous' would be gloating that their names and information weren't on that site. I don't think it is 'self-righteous' to be pleased in knowing my integrity was not compromised; that my wife and children can be secure in my fidelity to them. I do not gloat over the situation of these millions and believe that what the hackers did was a crime, but friends this is Living Wisdom in action. Integrity doesn't imply perfection, but rather that what we appear to be publically is truly who we are.

Those lacking integrity often care little about immoral thoughts and actions. Many connected to

---

[38] In case the reader is unaware, Ashley Madison is a 'service' that assists men and women in finding and carrying out extra marital affairs

the Ashley Madison breach were angry that they had been discovered and perhaps fearful of personal consequences, but how many truly regretted their actions and choices in a way that led to repentance[39] and a change of life? How many pointed the finger of blame at themselves and said, 'if I had been a person of character I never would have been on that site'? Living Wisdom is proven right: "no one is established by wickedness, but the root of the righteous will never be moved" (12:3).

Hypocrisy prevents me from being honest not only with others, but with myself. Hypocrisy blocks my ability to recognize my need for the Lord. Living Wisdom teaches me how to be a person of integrity in both my actions and my motives. With hypocrisy on its way out I again move towards the way of living well before the Lord.

~Emotions

Our emotions can be overwhelming and keeping emotions in check can be a challenge for many people. I do not believe that emotional struggles should be as debilitating as many make them out to be, but I have unfortunately observed how many people become the victims of 'self-inflicted suffering'. Let me explain this term.

---

[39] "Repentance is a complete 180 degree change of heart, mind and behavior. Saying we are 'sorry' is not repentance in the fullest sense necessary for salvation. True repentance comes from a heart broken by the knowledge that God has been offended by our sin and is followed by a commitment to turn away from such actions and attitudes."

I have observed in over 15 years in ministry a type of person trapped by their own choice to be trapped; perpetuating the problem. A person who is lonely refuses to take advantage of opportunities for fellowship. Another who bemoans their unemployment refuses to take a part time job. One in spiritual crisis will not seek the Lord in prayer or through the reading of the Word but say they are 'too busy'. These are people caught up in damaging behavior patterns such as addiction to alcohol or drugs or the abuse of food leading to obesity, high cholesterol, and heart disease yet refusing to seek real help for real change. I have observed that even many destructive thought patterns including certain types of depression are sustained by a person's willingness to live under their shadow.

All of this is 'self inflicted suffering'.

I have counseled those 'afflicted' with these challenges who choose not to seek to overcome them, but rather seem to take a twisted pleasure in their misery; they aren't 'happy' unless they are miserable, and making the people around them miserable as well. They are experts at playing the victim and passing blame for their condition. They spend countless hours and dollars on therapy when what they need is the real presence of Jesus in their lives.

These actions and attitudes are tragic no matter the person, but they are utterly heart breaking when they happen among Christians, for whom victory through the grace and power of Christ Jesus is available.

These words are difficult for me to write because they bring to the fore of my mind a friend who was beset by depression, anxiety and fear—much of it, self inflicted.

When I met Lou (not his real name) in 2012, he had already spent over a decade in professional counseling with very little to show for it. I spent many hours with Lou trying to help him understand some of the underlying spiritual issues which contributed to his struggles. Regrettably, my friend was unable and, in many ways, unwilling to take the positive steps which were suggested to him by the many who cared for him. While I do believe Lou received salvation through Jesus, he was sadly unable to discover wisdom. Lou remained a victim of self inflicted suffering until he took his own life in May 2015.

Sometimes the choices and situations of an unwise life have resulted in such overwhelming psychological chaos that discovering how to live a wise life is virtually impossible. The ingrained patterns of behavior, the damage caused by abuse or stresses or depression are so deep that it may require years to heal, and if those issues have caused intensely painful mental fractures, that person may never discover the wise life or the joy of Christ.

We all know that emotional pain is a reality of life and Proverbs is not ignorant of broken hearted people: "even in laughter the heart may ache, and the end of joy may be grief" (14:13). Friends going through difficult times may put on a brave face but we know they are torn up inside. At the same time we do not receive permission from God's Word to remain in a perpetual state of spiritually stunted gloom, always looking for the cloud behind any silver lining.

People who suffer from depression often cut themselves off from contact with friends or family feeling that their presence is a burden. But in doing so, they add the pain of loneliness. Even in the struggle of depression, Living Wisdom points the sufferer to the compassion and guidance of true friends: "Oil and perfume make the heart glad, and the sweetness of a friend comes from his earnest counsel" (Proverbs 27:9).

Friends and family are our greatest resource in times of emotional need. I include also the relationships within the Church, the family of faith. I plead with you, if you are a person who struggles with depression (as I myself have), don't try to cope alone; there are certainly people who love you, but you must be willing to take the necessary steps and reach out for the hand of help offered. You cannot cut yourself off from others and expect to overcome the challenges. Find a community to support and strengthen you. Do not suffer silently and do not inflict more suffering on yourself.

Emotions cloud our ability to find joy and peace. There is hope when we face those emotional tipping points. There is a great God Who loves us and desires to lift our burdens. We must reach out for the Living Wisdom that guides us into brighter days of living well before the Lord.

~The Abuse of Free Will

The Lord created man with free will, the ability to choose right or to do wrong; to be wise or foolish. Ministers, parents, teachers; you understand the frustration of knowing the right way which will lead those in our care to a wiser, happier life, but not having the power to make them follow, instead having to stand by helpless as they choose other paths.

In Proverbs 4:10-19 the pros and cons of the good and evil paths are set forth clearly. The good path leads to freedom and sure-footedness (4:12), while the evil path is the way of slavery to an all-controlling lust for sin (4:16). The good way is light (4:18) in which each choice becomes clearer than the one before. The evil way is utter darkness in which the one who walks it cannot even see the obstacles before them (4:19).

Each of us stands at the fork in the road, what Jesus later calls the 'wide and easy way' versus the 'narrow and hard way'. To complicate matters the choice is always before us, confronting us every day. Maybe deciding in favor of the right gets easier with each successive choice…maybe not.

Oswald Chambers commented,

> "God will not give us good habits, He will

not give us character, He will not make us walk aright. We have to do all that ourselves. To take the initiative is to make a beginning, to instruct yourself in the way you have to go."[40]

Moses challenged the people to "obey the commandments of [YAHWEH] your God" and find abundant life, warning them that disobedience would lead to exile and death (Deuteronomy 30:15-18). Joshua issued the well known challenge, "...choose this day whom you will serve..." (Joshua 24:15). Moses and Joshua had made their choices, but couldn't decide for the people; nor would God force the issue.

When we leave the freedom to choose open, we need to be prepared for the wrong choice to be made. After all, isn't that what happened in Eden? God set before the first couple a very simple choice: avoid the fruit of the tree of knowledge and live, or eat and die. It should have been obvious, but we know the choice they made.

Perhaps Solomon thought back on these things as he penned the words to his son. He had discovered the good path, but could not decide for his son. He can point to the right way, the way of wisdom, but ultimately cannot force his son to decide wisely; the decision to accept or reject the wise words of his guides is his alone to make. We

---

[40] Chambers, Oswald. *My Utmost for His Highest*. Barbour & Co. Inc.: Uhrichsville, OH, 1935, 1963. Print. p131

will see his choice later.

'Son', Solomon says. 'There's a good way to go; a way that leads to a happier, safer, more productive life. To ignore this way leads to disaster. Son, I can tell you which path you should choose, but I cannot make you choose it. But know this: if you decide to go the opposite way, the consequences are of your own doing; don't think that you can blame anyone else. So...what will it be?'

Exercising our free will to pursue sin will never allow us to grow as followers of the Lord. Living Wisdom teaches me how to exercise my will to choose the Lord's way, enabling me to live well before Him.

~Outward Challenges to Developing Wisdom

Just as there are inner causes which hinder the discovery and pursuit of wisdom, so there are external factors which weigh on us, unsettling our thoughts and minds. I offer these few for consideration.

~The Stress of Conflict

Life gets complicated.

Some of you have children going through the abrasiveness of their teen years. For others, there is difficulty in relationships and marriages. Still others are struggling at work. Whether it is in the home, the workplace or even in our churches, conflict can and does crop up anywhere there are people who disagree and act in selfish ways. We are thrust into stressful situations which affect how we think and feel.

Two of the most powerful forces in the world are water and wind. There is nothing we can do to stop either. Solomon warns us that conflict is "like letting out water" (17:14a); once it begins to run there is little to stop it, so "quit before the quarrel breaks out" (17:14b)

When conflict comes to us we can work to defuse the situation or we can aggravate the circumstances: "A soft answer turns away wrath, but a harsh word stirs up anger" (15:1). Reflecting honestly, we know that the majority of the time we choose to lash out with a harsh word or bitter comment. When has this ever made anything better?

The Hebrew word 'soft' (*rak*) carries the implication of tenderness or even weakness; to give the soft answer is to appear weak. Here we are faced with one of the greater challenges of Living Wisdom: to consider peace of more value than reputation. Am I willing to 'lose' an argument, even if I am right, in order to 'turn away wrath' or must I always win, even if it means that I 'stir up anger' and contribute to the conflict?

We cannot always control how or when these situations arise, but as people growing in Living Wisdom, we do have control over how we respond;

and while we do not always exercise this control, it is there nonetheless.

~*The Effects of Alcohol*

A young man graduates high school, excited for his achievement and the opportunities open before him. Later that night, after 'celebrating' with friends, the young man gets behind the wheel...you can fill in the rest. The young man goes to trial, faces convictions, and serves time in jail and suddenly his life looks much different than it did that moment he tossed his graduation cap into the air. This is not any one story in particular but is lamentably all too common and the key culprit is the misuse and abuse of alcohol or other addictive substances.

Scripture never forbids the use of alcohol[41]; rather it forbids drunkenness, violation of societal law (which would include underage drinking), irresponsibility and loss of self-control which drunkenness leads to. It is not alcohol which is evil, but its abuse; not having a drink in itself which is condemned, but the irrational pursuit of, addictive dependence on and overuse of 'wine and strong drink'. In these ways, alcohol is no companion of Living Wisdom.

Solomon reveals that he sought pleasure and satisfaction through the use of alcohol (Ecclesiastes 2:3) and came to the conclusion that "wine is a

---

[41] If the reader wishes a fuller explanation of this position they may email the author at comfaithnet@gmail.com.

mocker, strong drink a brawler, and whoever is led astray by it is not wise" (20:1).

He expands later in Proverbs 23:29, asking: "Who has woe? Who has sorrow? Who has strife? Who has complaining? Who has wounds without cause? Who has redness of eyes?" Who are those people for whom alcohol becomes a snare and an enemy; whose lives are turned upside down; whose families are devastated? It is "those who tarry long over wine; those who go to try mixed wine" (23:30). It is not those who enjoy a casual drink every so often, but the ones who 'tarry' (from the Hebrew *achar* meaning 'to linger for a long time') and who 'go' (*chaqar* 'to seek out') drink. For such people alcohol becomes an all consuming desire, even though it is ruining and poisoning them just as if they had been bitten by a venomous snake (23:32). In their forgetful stupor, through the pounding headache and the bleary eyes their thoughts are "I must have another drink" (23:35).

We know the many devastating effects on our communities and homes which result from the abuse of alcohol. We have heard the stories of lives torn apart by the actions of those under the influence. These are horrible and yet there is a greater disaster resulting from the over consumption of alcohol. The prophet Isaiah wrote:

> "Woe to those who rise early in the morning, that they may run after strong drink, who tarry late into the evening as wine inflames them! They have lyre and

> harp, tambourine and flute and wine at
> their feasts, but *they do not regard the deeds*
> *of the Lord, or see the work of his hands"*
> (Isaiah 5:11-12 my emphasis).

The abuse of alcohol has the capacity to completely derail the development of Living Wisdom because, as this passage points out, it prevents us from thinking about our need for wisdom and blinds us to wisdom's Source.

With all the damage it can cause, isn't it 'wise' to stay away from alcohol altogether? I cannot argue with that sentiment, but remind you that a choice of complete abstinence is based on personal conviction and preference, and while backed by solid principles is not necessarily equal to the Living Wisdom which we are exploring[42]. Total abstinence for its own sake, put forward as a demand for all to follow, is law. Abstinence put forward as a choice of personal conviction is wisdom. We must be on our guard against those who, even though well meaning, mistakenly substitute 'law' for 'wisdom'.

My friend Rick[43] was ensnared by alcohol. By God's good grace he is and has been for many years, sober. But he knows how that enemy can rear up to grab him again. He has said on several

---

[42] While I personally do not espouse total abstinence from alcohol I have the utmost respect for my brothers and sisters who do and I ask their forbearance if my comments make them uncomfortable; I in no way intend to challenge their convictions or decisions.

[43] Name used with permission

occasions, "If I have a drink today, I'll be mortgaging my house tomorrow." Living Wisdom has impressed on Rick the utter necessity to stay away from alcohol.

For those struggling with and overcoming addictions, Living Wisdom compels you to completely reject the use of alcohol, but on the whole, Living Wisdom does not lay a law of abstinence on us in matters of drink, but rather shows us a principle of moderation and self control. If I am to seek and find Living Wisdom it is to be with a mind unclouded by the negative effects of alcohol.

~Bad Company

Another influence in our lives which can lead us away from sound thinking and wise choices, discussed in part in the previous chapter, is poor choices of friends. Solomon observed the people around him and came to some conclusions about the company we keep: "Whoever walks with the wise becomes wise, but the companion of fools will suffer harm" (13:20). It seems straightforward enough, but not always easy to put into practice.

Growing up I had a good friend, I'll call him Jim. Jim was a year older than me but we shared similar interests. We loved fishing and being outside running through the woods, exploring the marshes and streams near our homes. As we went through grade school it became apparent that Jim had a growing propensity for poor decision making which got him into increasingly deeper trouble. One day Jim and another boy lit a fire in the hollow base of an old tree. You can guess the rest. I was with my father (who was as I stated earlier the town fire chief) and went with him to the fire call. Jim was in tears as the firemen questioned him.

After the fire, I seem to remember that Jim and I hung out less and less, which was difficult for me because we had such good times together. I see now that the Lord was protecting me even then with Living Wisdom. Not long after high school Jim got into drugs and was involved in some other questionable activity. Jim died of an overdose several years ago, a young man ruined by bad decisions.

Almost one thousand years after Solomon, the Apostle Paul offered a similar bit of advice to the Corinthians. Quoting from the Greek playwright Menander[44] he wrote: "Do not be deceived: 'Bad company ruins good morals'" (1 Corinthians 15:33). While he may have been specifically warning against false teachers in the Church, Paul understood this simple principle of Living Wisdom: the company we keep matters, so choose well.

~The Effects of Influences

All of these challenges discussed above have a

---

[44] Kaiser, Walter C. (Editor). *Archaeological Study Bible*. Zondervan: Grand Rapids, 2006. Print. p1881 note on Menander's *Thais*

definite effect not only on how we feel, but how we act.

~Temper, temper…

You wait patiently for a parking space and at the last minute, someone cuts you off and slides in. You run into the store for a loaf of bread and a soda, but the person ahead of you in the ten items or less checkout line is eight items over the limit, trying to redeem multiple coupons and cannot get their debit card to work in the scanner. You finish cleaning up after dinner and get ready to settle down for the night when your kid tells you he needs a book for a reading project in class…and it's due the next day (I actually did that to my mother!).

These types of situations get our blood boiling. We feel flushed and hot in the face; our jaws clench, our teeth grind as nasty thoughts race through our minds. Admit it; we've probably all been there. And oh it feels so good to let that steam blow! Well, for a second it does. Then the guilt sets in; we wonder how we could have let ourselves fly off the handle. We chastise ourselves for not being more controlled. Why can't we let it roll off us?

Solomon has quite a bit to tell us about our temper. We know how irrational we become when we get angry. Proverbs 14:17 warns us that "a man of quick temper acts foolishly". Too often we react only to regret. Living Wisdom calls us to learn how to control our temper: "Whoever is slow to anger is better than the mighty, and he who rules his spirit than he who takes a city" (16:32).

That's a pretty astounding comparison! Think of the great conquerors of history: Nebuchadnezzar, Alexander, Napoleon. You can be mightier than all of them combined…if you can learn to rule over your temperament! Have you ever had opportunity to blow your stack but you didn't? How did you feel? I've had a few moments like this and I can testify that I felt like I could leap over a house or run a marathon. But more important, I felt closer to the Lord, as if in that moment, He truly had the control I always tell Him I desire Him to have.

The letter of James, the New Testament's contribution to 'wisdom literature' picks up this theme:

> "My dear brothers, take note of this: Everyone should be quick to listen, slow to speak and slow to become angry, for man's anger does not bring about the righteous life that God desires" (James 1:19-20).

This is one of my 'go-to' verses when I feel that heat rising. I do want to be right before the Lord. I *do* want to live a life pleasing to Him. This is impossible if I give in to 'man's anger'. The term is literally the 'wrath of man'. Wrath in this case is the Greek word *orge* (or-gay); anger which breaks forth violently such as striking out verbally or physically. It's ugly and it's probable we've all done it. It is behavior that draws us away from God, making us 'fools', as Solomon points out: "Whoever is slow to anger has great understanding, but he who has a hasty temper exalts folly" (14:29)

Living Wisdom and a quick temper are not companions in any manner at all. This is a hard truth and I thank God for His forgiveness! I am also grateful that recognizing this truth is part of Living Wisdom trying to break through and take control.

~If You Can't Say Something Nice...

Proverbs tells us that "to make an apt answer is a joy to a man, and a word in season, how good it is" (15:23). This means that the right word at the right time has great power for good. The flipside is that the wrong word or even a good word at the wrong time can have disastrous effect.

When we lose sight of wisdom we often let loose against others, either because we blame them for our problems or perhaps we are looking for an outlet to keep from having to deal with our own mess. The negative influences affecting us bring out not only words of anger, but can also induce us towards more insidious types of speech. The number of proverbs dealing with our words and speech make a comprehensive discussion difficult, so I will mention just two common problems.

~*Gossip:* It is so easy to fall into this trap; we love

to dish it don't we? Sometimes we do it without thinking or even intending to; the thread of conversation leads down a path and suddenly we're telling tales.

I suppose this 'innocent' gossip can be forgiven more readily than the type of which Proverbs warns us against—those who take delight in spreading stories. The Bible calls them 'whisperers' (from the Hebrew *nirgan* meaning 'to slander'): "The words of a whisperer are like delicious morsels; they go down into the inner parts of the body" (18:8).

It is not without reason we call gossip 'juicy'. Like any other sin, it looks good at the outset. At first glance the second part of that proverb might seem positive, but if we think about it we realize that those juicy tidbits poison us from the inside out. We begin to accept gossip as normal or right; we don't stop to consider that the story may not be true; we begin to treat people different. Our moral character rots.

We could lay all the blame at the feet of the perpetrator, but the fact of the matter is that the one who listens is as much to blame and is counted as being as much in the wrong: "an evildoer listens to wicked lips, and a liar gives ear to a mischievous tongue" (17:4). Listen to gossip and you are branded by the Word of God as an evildoer and a liar. Yikes! That puts my willingness to listen to tales in a totally different light.

Living Wisdom leads me first of all to keep a

confidence: "he who is trustworthy in spirit keeps a thing covered" (11:13); and secondly to stop a gossip in their tracks, as Solomon wisely related: "for lack of wood the fire goes out, and where there is no whisperer, quarreling ceases" (26:20).

Confront a gossip with their sin, expose them and then walk away from them; leave them with no one to tell their stories to and the fire will go out.

~*Sarcasm:* A quick wit is a delightful quality; I appreciate someone who brings levity to a situation. I think we can even in good fun 'roast' one another. There is, though, a type of humor which is cutting, hurtful and destructive.

It is true that the wisdom literature does not use the word 'sarcasm', but the implications are present. Solomon writes that "gracious words are like a honeycomb, sweetness to the soul and health to the body" (16:24). The inverse of this is that discourteous words are bitter and poisonous. As another example: "a gentle tongue is a tree of life, but perverseness in it breaks the spirit" (15:4). When we use sarcasm for the purpose of tearing someone down we do in fact cause damage to a person's spirit, unsettle and unbalance their mind which in turn can lead to physical symptoms.

Living Wisdom tells me that "the heart of the wise makes his speech judicious and adds persuasiveness to his lips" (16:23) and that "the lips of the righteous know what is acceptable" (10:32). A wise person knows where the line is and has the self-control not to cross it. A wise person sees when damage has been done and seeks to bring healing.

~The Wisdom of Silence

Perhaps you are familiar with a 'proverbial' saying often attributed to Abraham Lincoln or Mark Twain (though probably belonging to neither): "Better to remain silent and be thought a fool than to speak and to remove all doubt." This expresses an important principle as we consider the use of our words: people led by Living Wisdom know when to speak and when to keep silent.

Wise people think before they speak, measuring their words: "The heart of the righteous ponders how to answer" (15:28). Wise people speak concisely and precisely: "When words are many, transgression is not lacking, but whoever restrains his lips is prudent" (10:19). Wise people know that fewer words do more to reveal their true character: "Whoever restrains his words has knowledge, and he who has a cool spirit is a man of understanding" (17:27).

There are many people who cannot stand silence. If there is opportunity to talk, they will take it. Yet Living Wisdom teaches us that sometimes the best thing we can say is nothing at all.

*

With all the negative influences assailing us Living Wisdom points to a path by which we may navigate a course of peace and health, guiding us in how we think and the way those thought processes influence how we behave.

As you probably know all too well, it doesn't take much to push us over the edge; to unsettle our hearts and create turmoil within us. This inner storm too often erupts outwardly in angry and bitter actions or words. We must become masters of our hearts, which I know is easier said than done. Truly God's words to Cain apply to us all:

> "...sin is crouching at the door. Its desire is for you, but you must rule over it" (Genesis 4:7).

Living Wisdom makes the choice clear. So...what will it be?

Be Wise.

Chapter 5

TWO WOMEN

An interesting feature of Proverbs is the personification of wisdom as a woman. We briefly met 'Lady Wisdom' in chapter 2 as she added her voice alongside Solomon. There is another woman present in Proverbs and set in contrast to Lady Wisdom. As being enticed to follow the ways of this woman are one of the heights of foolishness, we will refer to her, following the lead of other commentators, as 'Madame Folly'[45].

In chapters two through seven in the ESV she is named four times as 'the adulteress' and four times

---

[45] Kidner p21. It is important to note that although the passages being examined focus on men falling into sexual sin, the principles apply to women as well. Sexual immorality comes to women perhaps as 'Mister Folly'.

as the 'forbidden woman'. She emerges at several points in these early chapters in connection almost entirely with some form of sexually immoral activity. As such Madame Folly and her allures are grave threats to wisdom.

It is through the presentation of these two women that we are given the majority of Living Wisdom's teaching regarding sexuality and sexual ethics. They represent opposite and competing poles, one standing for life the other death; one good, the other evil.

Although I had read through Proverbs several times, it did not strike me immediately that there was little to nothing said about sexuality after chapter 9. Could it be because this subject is too important to reduce to 'simple' proverbial sayings? Does God wish us to know that a person who acts as a fool in their sexuality cannot ever be truly wise in the other aspects of their life?

While some readers may find this to be an uncomfortable topic it is essential that Christians be able to speak frankly and honestly about sexual ethics and morality. It is clear from the conditions of our culture that God's Living Wisdom in this area has been too long ignored.

~Madame Folly

Madame Folly appears early in Solomon's challenges to his son. In Proverbs 2:16-19 we discover that the adulteress is a "forbidden woman" (2:16); literally she is a 'stranger' or 'foreigner', not ethnically, but rather that she is an outsider to the covenant[46] of marriage between husband and wife.

By her "smooth words" (2:16), she flatters her 'victims', enticing them to join her as she "forsakes the companion of her youth" (2:17); the husband she was joined to when she was of marriageable age. Because marriage is a binding agreement made before God, her actions indicate not only an abandonment of her vow to a man, but that of a promise to God as well (2:17). This reflects the seriousness which marriage vows ought to hold.

Although in the days of ancient Israel marriages were arranged by the fathers and were often economically driven[47], this did not lessen the seriousness of the vows between the couple. Marriage vows are intended to be permanent and only in the gravest of circumstances are they to be broken by anything except death (see Romans 7:2-3).

Madame Folly appeals to a person's sense of individualism; their perceived freedom to decide

---

[46] A covenant is a strongly binding and enduring agreement between two parties, usually entered into by some form of religious ceremony. Geerhardus Vos remarks that "the outstanding characteristic of a [covenant] is its unalterableness, its certainty [and] its eternally validity." (Vos, Geerhardus. *Biblical Theology*. Wm. B. Eerdmans Publishing Co.: Grand Rapids, MI, 1971 seventh printing. Print. p33.)
[47] Matthews, Victor H., *Manners and Customs of the Bible*. Hendrickson: Peabody MA, 1993. Print. p20ff.; Miller, Madeleine S. & J. Lane. *Harper's Encyclopedia of Bible Life*. Castle Books. Edison, NJ, 1996. Print. p98ff.

who to be with, and under what circumstances. She speaks of marriage as an outdated concept; just a 'piece of paper', claiming that one partner is not natural and people should explore other options. Whatever argument she uses, the simple minded are swayed and follow her into paths of destructive behaviors. Proverbs 2 warns that "her house sinks down to death, and her paths to the departed; none who go to her come back, nor do they regain the paths of life" (2:18-19).

Of all the types of sin we can fall into, perhaps there are none as completely devastating as that which breaches the marriage commitment. Marriages that can survive unfaithfulness when it is a onetime incident are truly strong, but few are so strong as to survive multiple indiscretions, especially those perpetrated without regret or repentance. The passage warns that people who commit adultery with impunity are demonstrating a heart untouched by the wisdom of God.

In Proverbs 5:1-14 & 20-23 Solomon points to the devious nature of Madame Folly and the need for constant watchfulness: "My son, be attentive to my wisdom; incline your ear to my understanding" (5:1).

If you have ever observed a resting cat you notice that their ears seem to always be in motion, twitching at the slightest sounds. Not everything they hear is good and sometimes they catch the sounds of danger; but their ears instinctively tremble to catch the sound more clearly. When

Solomon speaks of the 'forbidden woman' he implores his son to 'perk up his ears'.

The words Madame Folly speaks sound wonderful, like dripping honey and smooth oil. Understanding how the ancients used these substances paints a clearer picture of what Solomon is saying. Honey was the primary sweetener of the ancient world (no sugar) and was also an antibacterial agent used in medicine to prevent and heal infections. Oil from olives is versatile; used for lighting lamps, cooking food and also for medical purposes. Olive oil is 'biostatic' meaning is does not spoil. It was used on burns and cuts and was applied before dressing a wound to keep the bandage from sticking.

Knowing this, we grasp the depth of Solomon's imagery. Madame Folly makes every word sound good and right, pleasant and soothing; however, she will not bring health, but death. The final end of her enticements is 'wormwood', a bitter, poisonous and deadly plant, and a razor sharp sword. "Her feet go down to death; her steps follow the path to Sheol" (5:5).

The sad truth about Madame Folly is that although she seems so in control, she is as ignorant as those who fall in with her: "she does not ponder the path of life; her ways wander, and she does not know it" (5:6). While it is clear that the woman acts deliberately, she gives no thought as to the final outcome or consequence. This is the tragedy of those who fall into sexual immorality, particularly adulterous affairs; they do not think beyond the supposed thrill and pleasure of the encounter. They do not consider the upheaval of lives that inevitably occurs when they are found out. They seek to justify their actions or brush them off as no big deal, but never admit or accept fault.

In Proverbs 7 Solomon relates what was perhaps an actual experience. He sees a man without sense, with no real convictions; a man who has not defined his moral boundaries. This senseless man walks down a street that runs closest to the home of a woman he knows to be of questionable character (7:6-9). Was it accidental or does he choose that street intentionally? How many can speak from experience that you have deliberately placed yourself in dangerous proximity to sin? I regretfully can attest to this. We slide in close to sin, hoping to feel a bit of its heat, but trying not to get so near that we get scorched. Invariably, like the mythical Icarus, we get too close and fall, just as this young man does.

The woman is out and about, looking for a target (7:10). She sees the young man and sensing his true desire, she pounces. Grabbing him she presses her lips to his and whispers in his ear, "I had to offer sacrifices, and today I have paid my vows; so now I have come out to meet you, to seek you eagerly, and I have found you" (7:14-15).

Many ministers bemoan the hypocrisy of the 'Sunday only saint' the countless people who play religion one day a week but have no intent of being changed by what they hear. The problem is an ancient one. This woman has been in the Temple, dabbling in a 'religion' which meant nothing to her. Her true religion is revealed to be an insatiable appetite for illicit sex. She entices the young fool with what awaits him inside her home; beautiful furnishings, comfortable sheets, a perfumed bedroom... and no husband to catch them in the act.

My mind goes back to another promiscuous woman in the Old Testament: The account in Genesis 39 of Potiphar's wife. Day after day she attempted to seduce young Joseph into her bed and day after day he resisted. Finally, when she physically attacked him, he fled from her as fast as he could.

Joseph had the correct response to the enticement of such a person, but the young man Solomon sees from his window seems to have no sense. Instead of fleeing, he gives into the "seductive speech" of the woman, following her for what he imagines will be the night of his life. Solomon's analysis is much different. The young man goes "as an ox goes to the slaughter, or as a stag is caught fast till an arrow pierces its liver; as a bird rushes into a snare" (7:22-23). He took the bait without realizing "it will cost him his life" (7:23).

Wisdom weeps for this young man, lost and destroyed by his inability to refuse sin; thinking only of immediate worldly pleasure rather than long term spiritual and emotional consequences.

Living Wisdom makes its message clear: it isn't worth it. Considering the outcomes, it is better to get as far away from Madame Folly as fast as possible; keeping clear of the places she is found (5:8). Don't waste your life, your energy, your honor or reputation by falling in with this woman.

In Proverbs 6:20-35 Solomon again urges the heeding of a parent's wisdom: "My son, keep your father's commandment, and forsake not your mother's teaching" (6:20)[48]. He goes on to speak of how the wisdom of a parent, sometimes learned the hard way, can spare the child from the difficulties which arise from poor choices. In these verses the parental encouragement has a specific purpose: "to preserve you from the evil woman, from the smooth tongue of the adulteress" (6:24).

We know the heartache and devastation that sexual misconduct has on a spouse and children in the home but we cannot forget the pain of the parents. The goal of a parent is to make their children better than themselves and when a child fails, parents are affected. The parents of the offended spouse may experience anger and grief that their child and grandchildren must endure the agony of betrayal. For the parents of the offender there is perhaps shame or guilt that their child has done such a thing as it may cast a shadow over

---

[48] I am impressed by the frankness by which the father speaks to his son on these matters. How critical it is, and how neglected, that the wise parent be open and honest in dealing with their children about sexuality and its attending ethics.

their parenting. If Solomon's son will listen to his parents everyone can avoid all that suffering.

If I may speak boldly, the Lord intends for sexual intercourse to be the most pleasurable and intimate thing a man and woman can share. The Bible refers to a couple in the act of sexual intercourse as becoming "one flesh" (Mark 10:8 e.g.). Is it then any wonder that satan works so intensely to corrupt this gift?

The allure of Madame Folly is strong: she is beautiful, she smells good and her clothing and jewelry provoke excitement. She offers all the pleasure of intimacy with no responsibility. But we are warned:

> "Do not desire her beauty in your heart, and do not let her capture you with her eyelashes; for the price of a prostitute is only a loaf of bread, but a married woman hunts down a precious life" (6:25-26).

This passage demonstrates that while prostitution is a serious sexual sin, sexual immorality between married people carries a far higher cost. As is usually the case prostitutes are unmarried women. The married person who turns against their marriage vow did not charge money for use of their body; but asked a far greater price in the destruction of lives and families.

The purity of women as virgins prior to marriage and then remaining chaste and faithful partners once wed was of great importance in

Hebrew culture[49]. This explains why the married woman who broke her pledge to her husband seems so vilified. But do not believe that the offending man is let off the hook! In 6:27 Solomon warns of the consequences to the adulterous man: "Can a man carry fire next to his chest and his clothes not be burned?" Adultery is like fire: play with it, even a little, and you will get burned. Thieves are expected to make restitution, no matter what their excuse for stealing (6:30-31), but the fury of a scorned and betrayed spouse can be intense and no payment can ever compensate for that violation (6:32-35). This is the inevitable fate of one "who goes in to his neighbor's wife; none who touches her will go unpunished" (6:29).

Once there were consequences for sexual immorality. People looked down on adultery and those who violated their marriage vows were not considered trustworthy people. Now the shame associated with adultery is quickly fading. It is expected. It is accepted. Often it is encouraged and even celebrated. Living Wisdom calls for a different way.

~Lady Wisdom

In stark contrast to Madame Folly, 'Lady Wisdom' is the voice of truth and reason; the voice of the Lord declaring the ways that are good and

---

[49] Matthews, Victor H, Benjamin Don C. *Social World of Ancient Israel 1250-587BCE.* Hendrickson: Peabody MA, 1993. Print. pp176-186

right. Lady Wisdom calls to all, seeking to raise them up; calling them not merely to just exist but to live to the fullest extent that God intends. It is in this tradition of life enabling truth that Jesus later says, "I came that they may have life and have it abundantly" (John 10:10). Lady Wisdom sees the world as it is but declares that it can be so much better.

In a previous chapter we discovered how Solomon began to expose the ploy of the sinner (1:10-19). That passage continues as he introduces his son to the alternative: "Wisdom cries aloud in the street..." (1:20), lifting her voice in an effort to sway the simple to lift the veil and embrace the right way. It is clear, as I commented previously, the call of wisdom goes out to all people. She is "in the street" and "in the markets", places where the people are. Perhaps this is the image underlying Jesus' statement to His disciples: "What I tell you in the dark, say in the light, and what you hear whispered, proclaim on the housetops" (Matthew 10:27). God's desire is for "all people to be saved and to come to the knowledge of the truth" (1 Timothy 2:4) and He does not withhold the offer of wisdom to anyone.

So why are so many pursuing the way of the fool? The answer lies in the following words: "How long, O simple ones, will you love being simple? How long will scoffers *delight* in their scoffing and fools hate knowledge?" (1:22 my emphasis)

It is a tragic reality that those so deeply in need of Lady Wisdom, are blissfully at ease in their stupidity. The simple love their simplicity, content in their naiveté and ignorance; scoffers delightfully choose their mocking ways; the fool hates knowledge; their pleasure in evil manifests in their persistence to do evil (1:22). The 'simple', having no sense of discernment, are easy targets and are effortlessly persuaded and seduced into evil. The 'scoffer' is one who scorns and mocks everything while the fool is morally bankrupt. They have no intention of hearing the call of wisdom and need little encouragement towards sin.

This rejection is not to be taken lightly. A key theme of Proverbs is the importance of gaining wisdom and associated with that are the serious consequences arising from rejecting the right way. We will discuss these consequences in a later chapter.

The awful refusal by certain types of people to lay hold of Living Wisdom should astound and sadden the tender heart of the Christian. The naïve reject wisdom in favor of stupidity; the scoffer in favor of their disdainful spirit; the fool for their folly. Scripture shows us the ugly nature of the grossly arrogant human heart which sits aloof from everything and mocks all things. Calling themselves 'intellectual' or 'modern' or 'progressive', they cannot see anything except their assumed superiority. They are so sure that no one has anything of value to offer them, so confident in their own grasp of reality and so clouded by their own haughty spirit that they miss the promise of Living Wisdom. Such are the type who, if they are not 'atheists', become Universalists, presuming that the compassion of God is too great to allow them to be lost. As it was in the days before the flood, it remains true that "...the wickedness of man [is] great in the earth, and...every intention of the thoughts of his heart [is] only evil continually" (Genesis 6:5).

Yet even in the face of such blatant rejection, Lady Wisdom continues to beckon: "...turn at my reproof..." (1:23). 'Reproof' is a corrective influence, sometimes painful if persistently refused. Reproof does not accommodate sin or coddle the sinner, but challenges them to face up to their ways and turn in the opposite direction.

For the soft and receptive heart which regards wisdom's admonition, a promise is given of a divine 'pouring': "behold, I will pour out[50] my spirit to you; I will make my words known to you" (1:23). This is an image the prophet Joel will use to speak of the Holy Spirit (Joel 2:28). Whether Solomon had in mind the fuller work of the Holy Spirit[51] or just a general spirit of understanding

---

[50] The word that is used here can also mean a 'bubbling up' or a 'flowing', representing an "uncontrollable or uncontrolled gushing forth [such as] the swollen waters of a wadi." (Harris, Archer, and Waltke p548)

[51] While the concept of the Holy Spirit was not alien to the Hebrew writers up to this point (see Genesis 6:3; Numbers 11:25; Psalm 51:11), the spirit spoken of in Proverbs would seem rather to be an

(Exodus 28:3) is not perhaps totally clear. Nevertheless, because wisdom is from God (Job 32:8) the 'spirit' promised is a divinely originated gift which will make the words of the Giver known to the receiver of the gift.

Let us not be misled; it is made plain that the gift is not unconditional nor is it to be held out indefinitely. Wisdom pleads with the wicked to stop and listen to her call; to turn from their destructive ways, but they persistently turn their backs, cover their ears, dig in their heels, and utterly refuse. They ignore and neglect what Lady Wisdom offers and because of these deliberate actions she withdraws her hand.

Worse yet Lady Wisdom becomes an enemy to the foolish and when disaster comes she will have the last laugh: "Because I have called and you refused to listen… because you have ignored all my counsel and would have none of my reproof, I also will laugh at your calamity…" (1:24-26).

When these days come, the foolish will look for the gift of divine wisdom to 'bail them out' but it will be removed far beyond their reach, silent to their pleading, hidden from their sight (1:28). Who then will they blame? Certainly they will look to cast the responsibility of fault on others or circumstances or bad fortune or even on God Himself, but in the end they can only blame the image staring back at them from a mirror.

---

enablement of understanding rather than the work of the Holy Spirit which brings what the New Testament calls the 'New Birth'.

"Because...*you* refused to listen...because *you* have ignored all my counsel and would have none of my reproof...Because *they* hated knowledge and did not choose the fear of [YAHWEH] ..." (1:24, 25, 29 my emphasis)

When one has rejected God, to whom or what can they call upon for help? What avenue of rescue is left to them? Truly "the simple are killed by their turning away...the complacency of fools destroys them" (1:32).

This is a hard pill to swallow for those who cannot or will not understand that God judges sin and oftentimes uses the very folly of the fool as their punishment: "they shall eat the fruit of their way, and have their fill of their own devices" (1:31). David spoke of this in Psalm 7:15-16: "[the wicked] makes a pit, digging it out, and falls into the hole that he has made. His mischief returns upon his own head, and on his own skull his violence descends." Solomon could see that the very method the wicked use to hurt others would be the means of their own destruction (1:32).

But doesn't God hear the prayer of the repentant sinner? Certainly He must or else none of us could be saved! However those spoken of here are not truly repentant and have no plan to turn from their sin; they just want a way out of the calamity and pain they have brought upon themselves. It is a false conversion with no real intent to change. As the wicked 'hate' (*sa'nay*- 'to become an enemy')

God, and have set themselves personally against His knowledge, it is impossible for them to heed His warnings.

An unnamed Psalmist[52] penned these lines: "Today, if you hear his voice, do not harden your hearts…" (Psalm 95:7-8). The time to heed the call of Lady Wisdom is *now*, before the catastrophes of life and the righteous judgment of God come to pass, because "whoever listens to me will dwell secure and will be at ease, without dread of disaster" (1:33).

*

None of us can escape the competing influences of these two 'women'; they continually call to us throughout our lives. They challenge us to develop discernment, to recognize good from evil and see through the false promises of any sinful behavior. As we grow in Living Wisdom, the voice of Madame Folly should become ever shriller and repugnant while the sweet voice of Lady Wisdom is more easily recognized.

As we heed Lady Wisdom, we should discover the peace and assurance of a life free from the fear of being tricked and overcome by evil. God's faithful followers in Christ still fall into the snares of the evil one and can be led into sin, but the general promise of Living Wisdom is that the life lived according to the principles of YAHWEH's Living Wisdom will be largely free from the foolish

---

[52] David according to the interpretation of this Psalm in Hebrews 4:7

choices and destructive results of Madame Folly. We continue to rely on the Spirit of the Lord and His gift of wisdom to lead us in a life well lived before the Lord.

Be Wise.

Chapter 6

LIVING WISDOM IN OUR HOMES

The previous chapters have set forth the importance and need of Living Wisdom. We have considered the source from which that wisdom flows as well as influences which may either guide or hinder our development. Now we turn our attention to some of the major arenas of life in which Living Wisdom must prevail in order for us to live well. The first of these is the home[53].

Because Living Wisdom begins in the home[54],

---

[53] The foundational community in which practically all people live is a family unit led by a father and mother. Scripture affirms the purpose of the Lord in creating the first parents as male and female, and joining them together, as man and woman, in a sacred relationship.
[54] Kidner p20

whatever threatens the home is treated with deep concern. Threats in Proverbs are living and breathing realities, not abstract concepts. Such threats may come from within in the form of rebellious children or quarrelsome spouses, or from without such as one who seduces a marriage partner into adultery or unfaithfulness. Living Wisdom exposes these threats.

Lady Wisdom continues to guide our discussion. She calls out to the simple and the wayward, promising them a way out of the death trap towards which the path of the sinner inexorably leads. She asks why they persist in following these deadly trails when they could have such a rich and happy life instead.

~Living Wisdom in Marriage

Marriage is a gift from God to His human creation. In that early narrative, Adam is found to be somehow 'incomplete', prompting the Creator to make for the man "a helper fit for him" (Genesis 2:18); accordingly God created 'woman'. God brought the woman to the man, who promptly serenaded her with the first love song (Genesis 2:23). The union of Adam and Eve was purposed by God to bring blessing to one another yet unfortunately, as the account unfolds, they betrayed one another, bringing heartache and imbalance to the relationship between men and women even to the present day.

We learn later in the Scripture that the union between one man and one woman in the covenant of marriage is intended to represent the spiritual union between Christ the husband and His Bride the Church (Ephesians 5:1-33). This representation gives marriage its high value and when marriage is devalued in any way, the beautiful picture of the Lord and His people is marred, blurred and lost.

~Sexuality in Marriage

As we considered, Living Wisdom informs us in our sexuality. Scripture is not ashamed of declaring the appropriateness of physical attraction and intimacy expressed appropriately between a husband and wife. The alternative to 'Madame Folly' is not the rejection or repression of sexuality, but a rediscovery and a delight in the physical and emotional love for one's spouse. In beautiful images, wisdom reveals this passion:

> "Drink water from your own cistern, flowing water from your own well. Should your springs be scattered abroad, streams of water in the streets? Let them be for yourself alone, and not for strangers with you. Let your fountain be blessed, and rejoice in the wife of your youth, a lovely deer, a graceful doe...be intoxicated always in her love" (5:15-19).

What a beautiful description of a young man captivated by his bride. In this passage Solomon reminds a young husband that all his desires are found in the woman he has pledged himself to. His intimacy is for her alone and hers for him. He is to "rejoice in the wife of [his] youth" (5:18) in contrast to 2:17 in which the adulteress "forsakes the companion of her youth". He is to be "intoxicated always in her love" (5:19) not by that of the adulteress (5:20).

Sometimes I see a couple who seem so different from one another, him tall and lean, her a stout woman; or her with the figure and grace of a model and he balding with a paunch. I wonder what brought them together and I remember that each sees beauty in different ways. No matter what someone on the outside thinks, to that couple, each is the most beautiful, most handsome person. When I met my wife she was seventeen and I was nineteen. As we age together, with all the attending physical changes that go with that process, I can tell you honestly that my wife is as beautiful to me today as she was the day we met; I remain truly captivated by 'the wife of my youth'.

Madame Folly is always placing images before our eyes and whispering in our ear to 'trade up', find someone younger, thinner, wealthier. She would like nothing better than to see a husband and wife betray one another sexually because when the sacred union is violated, corrupted or destroyed, living out wisdom becomes drastically more difficult.

Men and women, in the Name of the Lord I charge you: reject Madame Folly! Whether you are married or single, young or old, listen to Lady Wisdom. There is a reason Solomon framed the struggle in terms of life and death. Nothing has changed.

~Cooperation & Conflict in Marriage

A marriage can be menaced by threats other than sexual sin and infidelity. Issues of finances, parenting, job schedules and other matters can lead to a disharmony between husband and wife. Living Wisdom teaches husbands and wives how to work together, how to partner in their common purpose.

It is true that Solomon's culture was 'patriarchal'[55], but this concept has been misunderstood and miscast as an oppressive system in which women are devalued and subjugated. It cannot be denied that women were generally not afforded a high place in society; however the reality is that Hebrew and early Christian communities did more to liberate women than the surrounding cultures. The 'Evangelical Church' has been a liberating force for women in the face of social and religious forces including paganism, Romanism, humanism, eastern systems and Islam, all of which trap and enslave women[56].

While the primary role of women was oversight of domestic affairs, it was not a situation in which

---

[55] Matthews & Benjamin p23
[56] The actions of Boko Harem in Nigeria in 2014 is but one ongoing example of Islam's gross repression of women.

women were kept sequestered in the home as some type of indentured servant fit only to bear children and wait on her husband. In Hebrew culture women served in an essential capacity. While the men labored in the fields and served in the oversight and defense of the greater community, the women ordered and managed the home and educated the children: "In the world of ancient Israel, a man's home was his wife's castle. She had the domestic authority which he did not"[57].

Consequently Solomon can say with all seriousness: "He who finds a wife finds a good thing and obtains favor from [YAHWEH]" (18:22) and "house and wealth are inherited from fathers, but a prudent wife is from [YAHWEH]" (19:14). Because of her importance, "an excellent wife is the crown of her husband, but she who brings shame is like rottenness in his bones" (12:4).

Living Wisdom guides a husband and wife in working together as partners, respecting one another's gifts and talents and what each brings to their marriage. We are a long way past the age of men being the primary bread winner and women being the 'domestic engineer'. In our situation, my wife has generally earned the higher salary. This has never been a source of conflict and I have never denied her the opportunity to expand her skills in her field of work. She is the financial planner and organizer while I oversee much of the hands-on

---

[57] Matthews & Benjamin p25

household needs.

Ecclesiastes 4:9-12 describe the benefit of cooperation which applies to all of life and indeed to marriage. Conversely, Solomon lets us know in no uncertain terms the stress of a marriage soaked in conflict:

> "It is better to live in a corner of the housetop than in a house shared with a quarrelsome wife...A continual dripping on a rainy day and a quarrelsome wife are alike; to restrain her is to restrain the wind or to grasp oil in one's right hand" (21:9; 27:15-16)

When I read these verses I immediately see a 'hen-pecked' husband scampering out of the house, laying out a blanket and sleeping under the stars, in the rain, swatting the flies; anything to get away from *her*!

The nagging wife is likened to the incessant pit-pat of a leaky roof. Every 'drip' becomes more and more irritating and infuriating. The jaw clenches and the teeth grind—but-it-just-won't-stop! Dealing with that type of spouse is like holding back the wind with a screen or getting a grip on oil.

While men may relate to these sentiments, to be fair, we husbands can be just as difficult! It is likely because the wife had such responsibilities over the household that Solomon places the 'offense' on her. These vivid images reflect a picture of marriage in which the spouses are enemies, continuing that division which was unhappily introduced in Eden.

In the oft quoted (yet misapplied) text of Ephesians 5, the Apostle Paul lays out a plan by which a husband and wife function again as one in a relationship no longer based in the brokenness of the fall, but in the redeeming work of Jesus. As both husband and wife submit to the Lordship of Jesus, they willingly submit to one another in respect and sacrificial love. It is the discovery of this Living Wisdom which paves the way back to harmony and unity in marriage.

~*Living Wisdom in Parenting*

I have concluded that raising children is like being pecked to death by a duck.

Parenting is difficult; a slow, deliberate wearing down of patience and sanity. More than ever we need Living Wisdom to guide us in the raising of our children.

We have noted how Proverbs in particular is directed from a father to his son underscoring the important role of parents to pass on Living Wisdom to their children. Children also have responsibility towards the parent.

The command to "honor your father and your mother" (Exodus 20:12) is rooted in the stability of the ancient household. In the Hebrew household the father was more than just the sire of children; he was the provider and protector of all living in the home[58] while the mother was the teacher, a key guide for the faith development of the children. Additionally, the mother "had significant power and authority over decision-making and problem-solving for both land and children"[59].

It is due to these critical positions for the safety of the family and stability of household order that insult to parents was such a grave offense with dire consequence: "If one curses his father or his mother, his lamp will be put out in utter darkness" (20:20).

In contrast to most Western homes today, Hebrew households were bound by shared social and legal commitments and responsibilities; thus that command of honoring parents "expects the members of a household to fulfill concrete political expectations"[60]. As the children matured they took on responsibility for the health of the family. A child, specifically a son, who refused to contribute to the support and survival of the family, was considered a 'fool'. This son was far more than an embarrassment or annoyance to the family but became a clear and present threat to their reputation and survival in the community. If the son persisted in his foolishness and refused to heed the warnings of his parents, the entire community would be called to render judgment and in extreme cases could put the offender to death

---

[58] Ibid p8
[59] Ibid p23
[60] Ibid p11

(Deuteronomy 21:18-21).

Discipline is a sensitive topic in our culture due to the excesses and abuse perpetrated on children; but has the pendulum swung too far in the other direction making legitimate discipline a near impossibility with parents living under a shadow of fear of being reported to social services?

I know of a man for whom this fear was partially realized. He was in the grocery store with his wife and two small daughters when the older child decided to throw a tantrum. The man left his wife with the younger child to pay the bill, and took the older one out to the car. He strapped his child into the booster seat, shut the door and went around to the front, but before he could get in, the child had undone the buckle, opened the door and jumped out into the parking lot. Wrestling his daughter back into the car, he held her in the booster seat as she continued to scream. Later, back at home, there was a knock at the door. The pastor was mortified to find an officer of the local PD on his steps. Someone in the parking lot had seen him holding a screaming child in the car, but obviously not the entire scene, and called the police. Fortunately, the officer was very understanding when filled in on the situation. Nevertheless, the man was completely and utterly horrified as the potential headlines flashed through his mind.

The Hebrews had no such worries [61].

Proverbs 23:13-14 tells us, "Do not withhold discipline from a child; if you strike him with a rod, he will not die. If you strike him with the rod, you will save his soul from Sheol."

My folks had a twelve inch piece of 1x3 with something like 'spare the rod and spoil the child' printed on it. The threat of 'the stick' was usually enough to keep my brother and me in line. The above proverb recognizes that without discipline a person is headed for death and destruction.

Wise parents cannot ignore discipline. While we may no longer use a literal 'rod', the point of discipline is to correct behavior that will lead to trouble. Living Wisdom guides parents in the necessary and appropriate discipline for their kids, but does not let them off the hook to avoid carrying out that discipline.

~Train Up A Child...

Proverbs 22:6 might be among the most misunderstood passages in the Bible. The popular translation is rendered: "Train up a child in the way he should go; even when he is old he will not depart from it"[62].

---

[61] We must be cautious not to read our sensitivities into their culture, nor label them as cruel for their exercise of discipline.

[62] Most of the major translations such as the NIV, ESV, KJV & NAS follow this thought. The Darby Bible and Douay-Rheims follow the thought of this author as explained in the chapter. Additionally, other proverbial statements support this interpretation: "The rod and reproof give wisdom, but a child left to himself brings shame to his

That seems straightforward enough doesn't it? If parents can only provide the right atmosphere and pass on the right lessons, their kids will follow in those ways or at least come back to them later in life.

How many Christian parents have invoked these words as a type of incantation hoping to guarantee their children will turn out okay and remain in the faith if they provide the correct environment such as church or Sunday School? And how many parents were heartbroken when they discovered that such a statement is not a promise that our kids will walk in faith with the Lord. So what does this Proverb really say and how can understanding it help us avoid guilt and heartache over our children's decisions?

The verse is perhaps better rendered: 'Dedicate a child *to his own way* and when he is old he will not turn from it.' The commentary in the New English Translation says:

> "In the book of Proverbs there are only two ways that a person can go, the way of the wise or righteousness, and the way of the fool. One takes training, and the other does not...Train a child according to his evil inclinations (let him have his will) and he will continue in his evil way

---

mother" (29:15). "Folly is bound up in the heart of a child, but the rod of discipline drives it far from him" (22:15).

throughout life"[63] .

This means if parents allow their kids to be selfish, rude, etc., there is a good chance that they will continue these traits and habits as adults.

An experience from Solomon's own life bears out the truth of a child left to their own ways. As King David's life drew near the end, the time had come to pass the baton of leadership. Solomon had already been selected to follow David on the throne (see 1 Kings 1:30) but David's second born, Adonijah, proclaimed himself king. We read these words about Solomon's big brother:

> "Now Adonijah...exalted himself, saying, 'I will be king.' And he prepared for himself chariots and horsemen, and fifty men to run before him. *His father had never at any time displeased him* by asking, 'Why have you done thus and so?'" (1 Kings 1:5-6 my emphasis)

It seems that David had allowed Adonijah to have his own way continually from his childhood, and now, when strength of character was needed, Adonijah did not depart from his own way. Tragically Solomon was forced to have his brother killed to end the threat (2 Kings 2:23-25).

In the days of Solon of Greece, some 400 years after Solomon, it is reported that the Athenian council put a boy to death for animal cruelty. The

---

[63] The NET Bible®, ©1996-2006 Biblical Studies Press, L.L.C., Dallas, Texas; www.bible.org. Electronic Database; Biblesoft Inc.

reasoning of the council was that the actions of the boy were "evidence of a bad disposition; and if he was allowed to grow up, they would have greater and more serious trouble on his account"[64].

We can only speculate whether the wisdom tradition of Solomon had become known to the Greeks, but they seemed to understand that as this boy had been allowed to have his own way as a child, to let him carry such negative character into adulthood was a recipe for disaster.

Obviously I do not advocate killing children. I do wonder what type of society we will have in the next thirty years as more and more undisciplined and self-guided young people grow to adulthood.

It seems to me that the most important aspect of raising our children is maintaining a strong relationship with the Lord. I suppose in the end, no matter what mistakes I make as a father, so long as my children see a real and sustaining faith in me, that will be enough. Proverbs 14:26 says, "in the fear of [YAHWEH] one has strong confidence, and his children will have a refuge". If my kids know the Lord and grow to follow Him, I will rest easy.

While we cannot be guaranteed that our kids will turn out to be adults who live well before the Lord, as Christian parents we must take responsibility to mold and guide our children in the right ways. Living Wisdom demands we do!

---

[64] McKinstry, M. *The World's Great Empires*. Advent Christian Publications, Inc. & The Delmar Companies: Charlotte NC, 1973. Print. p120-121

*

Whether it is marital strife, rebellious children or external conflict, many influences trouble our homes. And yet there is more at stake than perhaps we have thought.

The Church is designed by God as a 'family of families' and the erosion of God's order for our households has a direct impact on the health of our local churches.

Since the 1960's, men have increasingly abandoned their homes and churches, either physically or by abdicating their responsibilities. Women have had little choice but to fill the voids. One writer who is keen to establish healthy families and churches writes:

> "Our families are fragmenting, authority is breaking down, and we are creating a generation of children devoid of all the benefits, character and security of stable family life in which men are leading their homes...Once a father's role as leader of the family is abandoned, all levels of family and community begin disintegrating." [65]

When the home collapses the Church is not far

---

[65] Reed, Jeff. *Belonging to a Family of Families: First Principles of Community Life.* LearnCorp: Ames IA 1997. Print. p32. Reed adds an important comment on our homes as they relate to the Church. Because the Church is this 'Family of families', when the families in a local congregation are in turmoil, it will be difficult for that local church to function effectively as Christ intends it to function.

behind.

I issue this challenge to Christian men: you must step forward and reclaim your Christ given role and responsibility as the leaders in your homes and your churches!

I issue this challenge to Christian women: you must be willing to step back and demand that your men rise up to restore God's order in your homes and churches.

I issue this challenge to leaders of local churches: it is critical that you assess the health of the households that comprise your congregations and do whatever is necessary to help every home be a healthy home.

For the sake of the testimony of Jesus Christ we must all renew our efforts towards the discovery and practice of Living Wisdom within our homes and families.

Be Wise.

Chapter 7

LIVING WISDOM IN OUR COMMUNITIES

Living most of my life in older New England communities, I was accustomed to independence when it came to my property. If I wanted to let my grass grow long, I could. If I wanted to put bushes along the front of the house, or tear up the lawn, I had relative freedom to do so. Moving to Florida, I was confronted with a new paradigm— the Home Owners Association. I cannot let my grass get too high; I cannot do any major work in the front areas of the property without having it vetted. This grates at my 'Live Free or Die' New Hampshire blood, but it is in some ways more closely related to the Hebrew idea of community. What one does, or does not do, affects those around us. A key difference is that while many HOA rules are designed to keep property values up and preserve an external sense of propriety, the interactions of households in the ancient Hebrew community were for survival.

The previous chapter considered the development of Living Wisdom in the home, but we cannot forget that our homes are part of a wider community; we must reflect on the impact of our family life on those within our community.

~No Man is an Island

God made humans to be social creatures and while we are not the only members of the 'animal' world to socialize, humans group themselves into communities which are unlike those of any other species.

Societies are built on the traditional family unit. These individual families gather into communities which expand from neighborhoods into towns and cities which group together into counties, then states and eventually a national structure. When any of these groupings, particularly the smaller units, are broken down societal balance is upset and the danger of collapse is heightened. We are certainly witnesses to this reality in our time.

In Solomon's day, the home was comprised of several generations living together in relatively close proximity. These individual homes combined together to form a village community. Marriages were carefully arranged for the health and harmony of the community. One cultural commentary notes: "Marriage customs among pastoral nomadic groups are often designed to maintain the social continuity as well as the perpetuation of the group"[66].

Contrasted with the modern West, in which every house lot is 'independent', the actions of individuals and households in ancient Israel impacted the entire village. We act in principle as islands unto ourselves and do not always stop and consider how our actions may strengthen or weaken the various communities we find ourselves a part of.

Relationships outside our home can be separated into a few categories; *socio-economic relationships* which include work related relationships, classified in Proverbs as those between masters and servants, as well as proper dealing in the 'marketplace', such as diligence and integrity in our work and dealing honestly and fairly with others; *governmental relationships*, including how we relate to and/or serve in positions of leadership; and *neighborhood relationships* dealing with our specific communities and groups in these communities such as local clubs or churches.

The wise person knows that living well within these various community settings is crucial to

---

[66] Matthews, *Manners and Customs* p20

stability and success.

~Living Wisdom in the 'Marketplace'

Village life in ancient Israel was centered on agricultural and pastoral activities or perhaps fishing for those settlements closer to the Sea of Galilee or on the Mediterranean coast. There were limited pottery, clothing and tool making 'industries' but these were enterprises based on local need with very few devoted specifically to these pursuits. Villages were largely self sufficient with each family unit filling a vital role and "harmony in the village was essential for the prosperity of its economy"[67].

As larger cities developed, the interconnectedness of the community would naturally decrease. Food was brought in from outside the city to feed a growing population of merchants, artisans and bureaucrats. The nature of cities draws in those who will not or cannot contribute to the needs of a smaller village. The old or crippled may gravitate to the cities where they can beg, while malcontents and those of questionable character might find success in thievery. Cities are also natural havens for those who deal in trade of a more disreputable nature.

The two spheres of life naturally intersected as the food provided by the villages was brought into

---

[67] Matthews & Benjamin, *Social World* p35

the city to be sold and products of the city purchased for the benefit of the villages. By Solomon's time, international commerce was being developed which added the new dimension of foreign influences and ideas. The marketplace was a hub of activity.

While modern neighborhoods no longer have quite the same economic interdependency, principles of Living Wisdom continue to guide our relationships and apply to us at our jobs and as we engage in daily buying and selling activities.

We have all stood in a line in a shop where the clerk just didn't seem to be able to make change on a dollar from a ninety-nine cent purchase. Or your server in a restaurant moved at a pace which would embarrass a sloth. Be honest, in these moments you do not think nice thoughts. However these are the exact times when we must demonstrate wise attitudes and actions in keeping with the pursuit of Living Wisdom.

Solomon tells us that "whoever is slow to anger has great understanding, but he who has a hasty temper exalts folly" (14:29). When you are standing in that line, you are face to face with the opportunity to show yourself as a person of wise character, or to show yourself a fool. I'm not saying it's easy, and I confess that I certainly need to work on this; however, the fact remains that how you conduct yourself will give a clue to others as to what type of person you are. Try to place yourself in the position of that clerk or server. Maybe it's their first week of work; maybe they just got news that their spouse was leaving them; maybe their child is ill. Does it really cost you to be kind? Nothing is gained from being rude, even if you feel you are being inconvenienced or not receiving the correct service.

I usually see the same woman working behind the counter at our local post office. I noticed on my first few visits that while she was efficient at her work, she was often curt with the customers. I figured out a trick. As soon as it is my turn I give a big smile and ask her how she is that day. I keep up a fun and friendly banter with her the entire time. What do I find? She is efficient and friendly. The Living Wisdom proves true: "A man who is kind benefits himself, but a cruel man hurts himself" (11:17).

Living Wisdom speaks to businesses owners/managers.

In ancient times dishonest merchants would rig their scales in order to cheat people and increase their own profit. Several times Solomon condemns this practice as repugnant to God (20:10 e.g.). The way you practice your business matters to God. Do you offer an honest price for your goods or services? If you are growing in Living Wisdom you will trust the Lord's provision and know that "better is a little with righteousness than great revenues with injustice" (16:8).

Living Wisdom asks how you treat those in your employ. Do you give them a fair wage? Do you make their working conditions pleasant? Do they feel that you value them as people? Proverbs 12:10 says, "whoever is righteous has regard for the life of his beast…" Now obviously I'm not saying employees should be viewed or treated as 'beasts', but a person developing Living Wisdom recognizes the great value of those who labor for them and treats them accordingly.

Living Wisdom also speaks to workers/employees.

In Ecclesiastes, Solomon came to some conclusions about work: "So I saw that there is nothing better than that a man should rejoice in his work, for that is his lot" (Ecclesiastes 3:21) and: "Whatever your hand finds to do, do it with your might" (Ecclesiastes 9:10).

A few questions come to mind: How do you approach your job? What is your attitude towards your supervisor or your fellow workers? If you are unhappy in your work, do you know why? What can you do to enjoy your work?

In 1996 I took a job in a poster and framing store in the local mall. I began at 7am on 'Black Friday' and was immediately thrust into the task of framing the pictures for customers. For 6 weeks, at just above minimum wage, I mounted pictures, and cut and assembled frames. I truly enjoyed that job! When the holiday rush was past, I was trained on the registers. A few months later I was promoted to 'second key' and a few months after that I was promoted to assistant manager, both with attending pay raises. When our manager left, it fell to me to oversee the store in the interim period. I did it all; opened and closed the store, hired new employees, made up the schedules, cashed out the registers and ordered supplies. What was it that put me into these increasing positions of responsibility? I came in on time, did my job well and tried to go above the basic requirements. I filled in for others when I could. I treated my co-workers well. Although I didn't know it then, I was walking out the principles of Living Wisdom.

Do you want to be known as a 'good employee' on whom the boss can count? Do you want to gain a raise in pay or a promotion? Work hard. Diligent effort will be recognized: "Do you see a man skillful in his work? He will stand before kings; he will not stand before obscure men" (22:29). The more effort we put into our daily work, the higher the chance that we will be recognized by those above us.

Proverbs 27:18 tells us that "whoever tends a fig tree will eat its fruit, and he who guards his master will be honored." The first part of the proverb indicates that you get out what you put in. If you go to your job complaining and withhold your best effort, you shouldn't expect a raise or a promotion or any other positive result. If you have a good attitude and are willing to go above the basic requirements you are more likely to find favor with those in charge.

The second part of the proverb tells us that a

servant, or in our culture an employee, has a responsibility to look out for the reputation of their employer; to defend them against backbiting and slander of coworkers. It is certain that such an employee would be held in esteem by their employer.

How we treat our co-workers is important. If you are like me there are certain people whom you work with or remember working with that you were glad to see on the shift roster with you, and equally there were those who were assigned that caused you to dread going into work. You want to be the former type of person whom others are glad to be working with because you bring a positive attitude to the job.

Whatever we do, Living Wisdom tells us to "commit [our] work to [YAHWEH], and [our] plans will be established" (Proverbs 16:3). When we devote our work to the Lord it will be natural to put the principles of Living Wisdom into practice; they will be the dominant characteristic noticed. But even if we are passed over for that promotion or not noticed for our work, we must still commit to the Lord's way.

As Paul would later say:

> "Whatever you do, work heartily, as for the Lord and not for men, knowing that from the Lord you will receive the inheritance as your reward. You are serving the Lord Christ" (Colossians 3:23-24).

In the end, it is not man's recognition which matters, but that we have lived well before the Lord.

Whether employer or employee, Living Wisdom identifies us to others as people who walk with integrity and set an example in our communities; people who care for the well being of all those they come into contact with.

~Living Wisdom for Community Leaders

Most reading this will never find themselves in the halls of power. You will never be a senator or governor or the President of the United States. But you will find yourself perhaps in a position of authority in your church or at your job; so as Solomon writes about kings and rulers, we can well apply the principles of Living Wisdom to whatever sphere of influence we are given.

Leadership is critical for the successful functioning of our communities, for "where there is no guidance, a people falls, but in an abundance of counselors there is safety" (11:14). Whether in our schools or our emergency services; our civic organizations or our local churches, when no one steps forward to take responsibility for the group, there will be a sense of aimlessness as everyone does their own thing.

As Solomon wrote of the wisdom of leadership, perhaps he recalled the history of Israel in the days of the Judges when "there was no king in Israel. Everyone did what was right in his own eyes" (Judges 17:6; 21:25). That was a dark period because what was right in the eyes of the people led them into sin.

Wise leaders know how to direct people along good and productive paths. They hold people accountable. Wise leaders surround themselves with counselors to give them guidance. With wise leadership the people know what their roles and responsibilities are; they know that they are a part of something bigger. I used to tell my congregation in Dover, NH that our goal was "everyone on an oar rowing in the same direction."

Of course this presupposes good and wise leaders. Unjust and unwise rulers were not unknown in the history of Israel. The pages of Scripture are speckled with the folly of such leaders; from the wickedness of the sons of Eli (1 Samuel 1-2) to King Saul's fall away from wisdom (1 Samuel 13ff.) and the evil kings who followed Solomon.

Solomon assumes the integrity of leaders who recognize that they are led by Living Wisdom: "By me kings reign, and rulers decree what is just; by me princes rule, and nobles, all who govern justly" (8:15-16).

Successful leadership begins with the search for and submission to the author of Living Wisdom. As reverence for the One True Lord is the origin of true wisdom, it is little wonder so many of our leaders, both political and 'religious', are weak and ineffective. Apart from the guidance of the Lord of Living Wisdom the decisions made by those in positions of leadership are based on man's desires of the moment rather than what is right and just. We elect leaders who are eloquent speakers, people of status or wealth, those successful in business or politics, but too rarely are we concerned with people of moral character and firm conviction who will lead apart from their own self interests.

What are the qualities of a wise leader who knows the Lord? Psalm 72, written by Solomon, is a prayer-song seeking YAHWEH's blessing on Israel's king. The psalm contains strong Messianic themes because the human king of Israel was supposed to be the representative of the divine King, though clearly they did not always live up to that calling. In the psalm Solomon describes the ideal wise king as having characteristics which should apply to all leaders, but must apply to those who lead among God's people. We are warranted in applying these qualities directly to those who lead the Church in Christ's Name.

~*The wise leader is just:* "Give the king your justice, O God...May he judge your people with righteousness, and your poor with justice!" (Psalm 72:1, 2)

The petition is for the king to be granted God's justice (*mishpat*) and righteousness (*tzadiq*) in order that he might then use those gifts on behalf of God's people. The wise leader seeks to be honest and trustworthy as he or she stands before the people to guide them in God's ways. Justice is paramount because it is rooted in the nature of God's dealings with His people.

~*The wise leader defends the needy:* "...he delivers the needy...the poor and him who has no helper. He has pity on the weak and the needy, and saves the lives of the needy" (Psalm 72:12, 13).

The king was intended to be the champion of the people. He was to be their deliverer and protector. Those who lead in God's ways should have a sensitive heart towards the weak. They are to be champions of 'social justice' according to the teaching of God's Word; to care for widows and orphans, to have compassion on the hurting and to defend those who cannot defend themselves[68]. The Church is not necessarily called to reform society on behalf of these people, but to bring them to Christ and into the family of Christians where they may find a loving and supportive community.

~*The wise leader develops and encourages a culture of righteousness:* "In his days may the righteous flourish, and peace abound, till the moon be no more!" (Psalm 72:7)

The king was to stand as a spiritual leader for the nation. We see this with but a handful of the kings of Judah in the accounts of Kings and Chronicles. Outstanding among these are Hezekiah and Josiah who undertook massive

---

[68] Refer to Exodus 22:21-27 as a starting point for this teaching

reforms to purge idolatry from among the Hebrews and lead them back to God' ways.

The purpose of a Christian leader is to guide people into a right relationship with God and with one another through Jesus Christ, and then to teach them how they are to relate to the unbelieving world around them with consistent faith. A Christian leader is deliberate about making their area of influence one in which Christian virtue and character is practiced and expected.

~*The wise leader oversees growth:* "May there be abundance of grain in the land...and may people blossom in the cities like the grass of the field!" (Psalm 72:16)

The king was responsible for the physical provision of the nation. God had promised plenty as blessing for obedience (Deuteronomy 7:12-14). As goes the leader so go the people. Hezekiah and Josiah were required to act drastically because previous kings had led the people away from God. The Christian leader desires *spiritual* growth[69] among the people he or she leads and can work towards this by modeling obedience.

~*The wise leader knows the Lord:* "Blessed be [YAHWEH], the God of Israel, who alone does wondrous things. Blessed be his glorious name forever; may the whole earth be filled with his

---

[69] It is unfortunate that 'successful' growth of a local church is more often tied to numerical increase—attendance and membership– rather than faith maturity.

glory! Amen and Amen!" (Psalm 72:18-19)

As the psalm concludes, Solomon celebrates YAHWEH as the One to Whom all praise is due. The king never acts in his own interests, but for the glory of God.

The ultimate characteristic of a good leader, one who is effective, strong and respected, is a leader who develops Living Wisdom based in a personal relationship with God through the provision of salvation and new life He has offered in Christ. The wise leader knows, reveres and obeys God.

~*Living Wisdom in our Neighborhoods*

We have been blessed, both in New Hampshire and in Florida, with some great neighbors; people we are glad to see when we are out in the yard or taking a walk; people who take the time to wave when they drive by or stop to say hello. We also live next to people who don't give us the time of day. Nevertheless these also are my 'neighbor' in the wider sense, and I still bear some responsibility for them.

Developing Living Wisdom is not merely some quest for personal spiritual betterment, but for the wider health of our communities. Proverbs 3:27-33 teaches us the benefits of Living Wisdom in our neighborhoods.

~Living Wisdom leads to a generous community: "Do not withhold good from those to whom it is due, when it is in your power to do it. Do not say

to your neighbor, 'Go, and come again, tomorrow I will give it'—when you have it with you" (3:27-28).

Wisdom informs a man to consider his neighbor's need and his own ability to meet that need. This is a principle rooted in the Mosaic Law in which the Israelites were warned against hard heartedness, and directed instead to be generous in meeting their neighbor's needs (Deuteronomy 15:8). This means more than throwing a few bucks into the Salvation Army pot at Christmastime or bringing some canned goods to the soup kitchen (and remember this principle: if *you* wouldn't eat it, don't donate it![70]). The principle of Living Wisdom at work here is relational; getting to know our neighbors, developing relationships with them so that they can count on us to be available to meet their needs as we are able. Living Wisdom calls us to generosity.

~Living Wisdom leads to a safe community: "Do not plan evil against your neighbor, who dwells trustingly beside you" (3:29).

Are our neighborhoods truly what that word implies? Are we really 'neighbors'? A neighbor is more than just someone whose house happens to be in close proximity to yours. A neighbor is someone with whom you are developing trust and friendship. A neighbor can knock on your door with the expectation of a warm and friendly welcome, and you can expect the same from them.

---

[70] Regards to Pastor Steve Aldrich for that tidbit!

When those living near us act in ways that bring tension or bad feelings, we say they are acting 'un-neighborly', but can that be said if there is not a sense of 'neighborliness' being built?

Living Wisdom tells us to care for our neighbor as if they lived in our home; to value their rights and property as much as we value our own (see Leviticus 6:2-4 and Deuteronomy 19:14 as well as Proverbs 23:10 & 22:28); to watch out for their best interests that they may feel secure. We know when we go away our neighbors will look after our home and we do the same for them. That is part of wisdom's teaching being lived out.

Every neighborhood has its malcontents, the people who are always complaining about something, making those around them miserable; Proverbs refers to them as those who run off at the mouth to belittle or destroy their neighbor' (11:9, 12). Many neighborhoods are confronted with the fear of 'gangs' and the pain of the poor, the lonely and the rejected. The one pursuing Living Wisdom develops an ability to recognize threats to true community and works to overcome them for "one who is righteous is a guide to his neighbor' (12:26). Living Wisdom gives us concern for our neighbors.

~*Living Wisdom leads to a peaceful community:* "Do not contend with a man for no reason, when he has done you no harm" (3:30).

We surely all know of those types of people who find great pleasure in intimidating or bullying others, to establish themselves as a person not to be crossed. This is *not* wisdom. Wisdom tells me that I am to live peacefully with people. Wisdom tells me to smile, to be gentle in spirit, word and deed. Wisdom tells me that being friendly is better than being a grump. Wisdom tells me to put people at ease in my presence as much as possible. If a person has not offended or harmed you, Living Wisdom says to treat them as a potential friend rather than an enemy, for "when a man's ways please YAHWEH, He makes even his enemies to be at peace with him" (16:7). Living Wisdom guides us to peace.

~Living Wisdom leads to a positive community: "Do not envy a man of violence and do not choose any of his ways" (3:31).

We see people prosper by means of violence, slander, theft and deceit and we instinctively realize that such behaviors are wrong. But sin never openly reveals either its true intention or its final end and, as we see these patterns renewed and repeated year after year, it is obvious that there are still plenty of people who "envy"[71] the wicked.

When we see people who would make their name at the point of a knife or the barrel of a gun, our response should not be envy, but pity, knowing that unless they change their ways they remain "an abomination to [YAHWEH]" (3:32) and under a "curse" (3:33)[72].

---

[71] Hebrew *qana*- 'to be provoked to jealousy'

[72] The Hebrew word *arar* commonly means something that renders one

For the follower of YAHWEH, all choices are to be weighed against the nature and character of God Himself. When a practice or pattern of behavior violates God's nature, Living Wisdom calls us to reject these actions and the unrepentant spirit that perpetuates them. The follower of the Lord, by contrast, can hope in the promise that "the upright are in his confidence" and that the Lord "blesses the dwelling of the righteous" (3:32, 33).

Living Wisdom identifies us to others as people who care about and seek to build healthy relationships in our communities. Living Wisdom directs our minds to the health and safety of our neighborhoods leading us to consider how to build a stronger sense of community as we begin to care for our neighbors as we do for ourselves.

~Living Wisdom for Community Health

Developing Living Wisdom for community life is not for our benefit. Two episodes from the days of David illustrate the wisdom of the wise benefiting the community. In 2 Samuel 14 and 20 we read of two wise women who acted to bring peace to the community threatened by division and strife. 1 Samuel 25 tells us the account of Abigail who also demonstrated wisdom which preserved the reputation of David as well as her own

---

helpless or fruitless; something that bans the one under the curse, as in Adam being banned from enjoying the productivity of the earth; so see Harris, Archer, and Waltke p168

household community. Impressed by such wisdom, David later took Abigail as one of his wives (1 Samuel 25:39-42).

Communities need strong leaders and Hebrew communities had ways to discover who those strong leaders were:

> "By the way they ate their meals, did not get drunk, worked hard, made good friends, sought advice before acting, held their temper, paid their taxes, and imposed fair legal judgments, the wise educated their villages to carry on successfully from one generation to the next"[73].

One way the ancient Israelite leaders kept order was by publically labeling those in the village. Those deemed as strong in the community could be openly designated by the elders with such terms as 'wise' or 'clean'—titles of honor. These were the people who could be counted on to work hard, serve in public office and bring good reputation to the village.

At the other end of the spectrum was the 'fool', who by his moral failure and destructive influence was a threat to the stability, peace and honor of a village or town. Those publically labeled 'foolish' or 'unclean' were shamed - and excluded from community life until such time as they demonstrated a change in behavior. This certainly

---

[73] Ibid p142

seems strange to us living in a culture which forbids passing such 'value judgments', but village stability demanded strong action.

For the unrepentant and intractable fool, much harsher punishment was set forth. Parents were given the right to bring their disruptive child before the village elders for judgment and in the most extreme cases, public execution (see Deuteronomy 21:18-21). Indeed by their unwise actions "fools endangered their very existence"[74].

In Hebrew culture these harsh responses were considered necessary to bring or maintain order in the community. Such action was intended not only to punish the offender but also serve as a lesson and warning to others who may be entertaining thoughts of similar antics.

Survival was bound up in the reputation of the home within the wider community and the reputation of that community among the others around them; one or two disruptive elements were a grave threat. Our modern sense of individuality and relativism which moves people to do that which seems right to them is brought up face to face with the Truth of Living Wisdom: "there is a way that seems right to a man, but its end is the way to death" (14:12).

We read of several instances in the life of Israel in which one village/city or even an entire tribe was attacked in response to their 'foolish' behavior.

---

[74] Ibid

One of the most extreme is found in the book of Judges in which the concubine of a Levite was set upon by a mob of Benjamites and died as a result of her abuse. The Levite sent out a call for the remaining tribes to go to war against the tribe of Benjamin to "purge evil from Israel" (Judges 20:13). The national community had been disgraced and the perpetrators had to be dealt with.

The desire of the community for justice and order is expressed in these wise sayings: "When it goes well with the righteous, the city rejoices, and when the wicked perish there are shouts of gladness" (11:10); and, "Righteousness exalts a nation, but sin is a reproach to any people" (14:34).

A wise community will recognize that its reputation and well being is dependent upon whether the 'righteous' or the 'wicked' are in the majority. A well ordered community, a neighborhood that you feel safe in, is one in which good people take responsibility not only for their actions but the actions of those around them. There is a shared sense of duty for the well being of their neighbors. A foolish community lets the disreputable and disruptive have free reign. Once opened, that 'Pandora's box' is very difficult to close again.

Leaders lead, even when that leadership is difficult or unpopular. Social stability depends on some sense of order, otherwise there is lawlessness and chaos such as were seen in the riots in Ferguson, Missouri (2014) or Baltimore, Maryland

(2015) or what was witnessed in some of the 'occupy' movements of 2011. While legitimate concerns may have led to those events, the way they were carried out was wrong, led by fools. When we become wise, we step forward to lead in ways that are beneficial to the community and that leadership becomes evident.

*

A community comes in many forms such as a neighborhood or a workplace, a social group or a local church. It is my hope that you will begin thinking in a new or different way about your place in those communities of which you are a part. If you are a believer in the Lord Jesus, you are in a vital position to be the voice of Living Wisdom to those who live and move within your communities.

Wisdom has issued a challenge for you to lead? Will you accept?

Be Wise.

Chapter 8

LIVING WISDOM & OUR RESOURCES

The Bible speaks quite a lot about money and possessions and offers a great deal of Living Wisdom when it comes to related issues such as earning and spending, saving and sharing and being good stewards.

I recall someone saying that our bank statements are some of the most revealing theological documents we possess. What a person does with their finances, how they relate to their material things, speaks volumes about their character as well as their view of and relationship to the Lord.

It seems evident that many Christians are not living well in terms of their finances. There is a certain amount of justification in blaming a broken political-economic system in which the value of currency falls while prices and taxes increase. However there is also the reality that so many have bought into a materialistic worldview which drives the chase for 'stuff' and sinks them into deeper debt. Our finances are a critical area in which we have ignored Living Wisdom.

~Living Wisdom for Our Daily Work

Unless you plan to renounce all material possessions and begin the life of a hermit, money is going to factor into your life.

The movie *The Wedding Singer* stars Adam Sandler and Drew Barrymore. In one scene Sandler's character, Robbie Hart, who makes his living as a singer at various local social functions, goes into a bank hoping for a more stable and prominent job.

When the bank manager asks Robbie why he wants to work at the bank he replies, "I'm a big fan of money. I like it; I use it; I have a little. I keep it in a jar on top of my refrigerator. I'd like to put more in that jar. That's where you come in"[75].

For the great majority of us who have not gained money through inheritance or the lottery, it is incumbent on us to work, in some form, to earn a wage. Whether you work as a laborer or in an office, as a teacher, in a shop or at a writing desk,

---

[75] Quote obtained from imdb.com; *The Wedding Singer*: 1998 New Line Cinema

the basic principle is a wage for a service[76].

Scripture affirms the value and honor of work from the very beginning of the world. After his creation, Adam was placed in the Garden of Eden and commissioned "to cultivate it and guard it" (Genesis 2:15 Good News Translation). Work became burdensome only after the fall of the first parents into sin (Genesis 3:17-19).

Proverbs continues this tradition of the value of work and the attending benefits to those who are diligent in their labor.

~The Wisdom of the Ant

A feature of the wisdom tradition is to learn the lessons that the created order provide. Job uses the patterns of nature to defend himself against his 'friends' (Job 12:7-8) and the natural world furnished the Lord Jesus with many object lessons (e.g. Matthew 6:26).

Solomon utilized nature as well: "Go to the ant, O sluggard; consider her ways, and be wise" (6:6). Have you ever watched an ant colony at work? It is fascinating—unless they are fire ants, in which case they are just a nuisance. Solomon, the great naturalist, obviously spent ample time crouching over an anthill; observing it from all angles, perhaps carefully digging down to catch a glimpse of the inner workings of the mound. Notice what

---

[76] For the hard working homemaker, while there is no weekly paycheck, your work is no less valuable, nor are you exempt from the principles of Living Wisdom.

he observed: "Without having any chief, officer, or ruler, she prepares her bread in summer and gathers her food in harvest" (6:7-8).

The ant knows what is required for survival; that food must be gathered, prepared and stored at the appropriate time, before winter sets in. The ant knows by instinct that it must work; that the colony cannot survive unless each member does its part. No one has to give the ant a job description or make sure it doesn't exceed its 15 minute coffee break. It works because it must.

Solomon turns that lesson back on the person who believes that they are entitled to the means of survival without investing their energy to contribute. The 'sluggard'[77] is a person who loves the easy life; sleeping late and lounging about all day. Not just on a sunny Saturday, but every day.

> "How long will you lie there, O sluggard? When will you arise from your sleep? A little sleep, a little slumber, a little folding of the hands to rest, and poverty will come upon you like a robber...want like an armed man" (6:9-11).

Solomon gives no notion that the sluggard can suppose someone will pick him up when he is down. No one is coming to bail him out. He causes his own problems and therefore should expect to deal with the consequences[78].

---

[77] From the Hebrew word *atsal* meaning 'to lean idly' or 'indolence'
[78] This sticks pins into the balloon of any welfare system in which those

Surely you know someone with a strong 'work ethic'; a person who gets up and gets to the job at hand; focusing on doing it right, doing it well and seeing that it gets done. That is a person with Living Wisdom.

Most have heard Aesop's fable of the ant and the grasshopper in which the industrious ant labors to provide and prepare for winter while the grasshopper fiddles the days away. When winter comes, the ant is safe and warm and fed while the grasshopper finds itself hungry and frozen. The Living Wisdom of Proverbs praises diligence and offers strong warnings for those who choose an indolent and lazy life.

We must once again take note of the culture and life situation into which the proverbs were spoken. In a largely subsistence economy, one in which each family could expect to eat only what they grew in the fields or raised in their flocks, there was no toleration for those who would not contribute. We read: "He who gathers in summer is a prudent son, but he who sleeps in harvest is a son who brings shame" (10:5; see also 12:11 and 20:4).

A person who did not invest his time and labor to prepare and plant his field or vineyard should not expect to magically discover a crop! Standing at the edge of a barren field while those who labored feasted on the bounty of their effort, selling the extras for a profit, they would realize the truth

who are able to contribute refuse and are not required to do so.

that, "A slack hand causes poverty, but the hand of the diligent makes rich" (10:4); "Slothfulness casts into a deep sleep, and an idle person will suffer hunger" (19:15).

There is no cruelty in these remarks, just a statement of fact. Rightly did the Apostle Paul lay out the same principle for the Church many years later: "If anyone is not willing to work, let him not eat" (2 Thessalonians 3:10).

Living Wisdom does not dismiss charity and compassion for those who are un-*able* to work (the sick, the elderly, etc) but rather rebukes those who are un-*willing* to work. I personally believe in the principle of a 'safety net' for such as are not able to contribute, but I am convinced that this is the responsibility of a town or city as it finds genuine need within its limits; not a state or national government with no understanding of local needs.

It must be admitted that we live in a culture where it is increasingly espoused that healthy and able people, should be given whatever they ask or want with no expectation of labor in return; a culture which rewards sloth and punishes labor. Such a concept was not unknown in the days of Solomon, but it was certainly not celebrated.

There are broad reaching consequences when the Living Wisdom of the Scriptures, which elevates the place of daily work, celebrates diligence and warns against indolence and idleness has been cast aside and forgotten.

~Keeping Perspective

Living Wisdom causes us to understand that our daily work is just one part of our total life. We cannot neglect the health of our families, our bodies or our spirits for the sake of our work, nor can we ignore the work of ministry which benefits the spiritual life of others. We must develop some different perspectives about money and possessions.

One of the quickest ways for Living Wisdom to be evident in our daily work is to put forth our best effort *with integrity*. The economic system under which Solomon lived was based primarily on sale and trade of goods and services. The farmer bringing his crop to market needed a fair and honest price, but there have always been those who look to profit at the expense of another, and so the greedy and corrupt in the market would falsify their weights in order to pay less and get more. The Lord explicitly built into the Law this prescription: "You shall have just balances, just weights, a just ephah, and a just hin: I am [YAHWEH] your God, who brought you out of the land of Egypt" (Leviticus 19:36). Proverbs upholds this: "A false balance is an abomination to [YAHWEH], but a just weight is his delight" (11:1). Living Wisdom demands integrity. We cannot 'gain our bread by deceit' (20:17) and expect to be considered wise, expect to be respected, expect to be blessed.

Whether you find yourself in a corner office on the top floor or standing over a dish sink; selling magazines, sweeping floors, driving a bus or managing an office; an honest day's wage for an honest day's work is nothing to be ashamed of or looked down on. To those committed to diligence, the guiding principle on which we lean is that there is a reward for the effort put forth in our daily work. A worker should be content with their wages. If not, we are fortunate that we may seek the means of a raise or may find other employment; but we must be careful that we do not do so just to make more money for its own sake.

As we work, we must remember always that our hope is not found in our bank accounts. Truly, "whoever trusts in his riches will fall, but the righteous will flourish like a green leaf" (11:28), for "riches do not profit in the day of wrath, but righteousness delivers from death" (11:4). There are greater matters than money which should dominate our concerns. Keeping this reality in mind should allow us to look at our money and possessions in a different way, a wise way.

We believe that all things belong to God and it is ultimately from His Hand that we have our daily bread and our possessions and therefore we have a responsibility to use these for His glory.

When we can recognize that money is not the ultimate goal of life, we find it becomes easier to let it go or to turn it towards other purposes rather than just increasing personal wealth. How we view and use our money and possessions is called 'stewardship'.

Stewardship comes from a compound Greek word which loosely translated means 'the law of the house' or the oversight of household affairs. To be a steward is to take the responsibility of overseeing the management of something. Financial stewardship means overseeing the proper collection and use of monetary resources. Living Wisdom instructs us in how to be responsible stewards and overseers of that which God has entrusted to us.

~Doing Good

Living Wisdom demands that we look beyond ourselves. The Scripture does not teach Socialism or Communism, or any other 'ism' for that matter, all of which come through the authoritarian demand of human government. What God's Word does teach is the principle of social concern and community welfare based on the recognition of God's sovereignty and the dignity of every human being.

Coming back to a portion of Proverbs 3:

> "Do not withhold good from those to whom it is due, when it is in your power to do it. Do not say to your neighbor, 'Go, and come again, tomorrow I will give it' — when you have it with you" (3:27-28).

Living Wisdom teaches us that when we have

the ability and opportunity to help a fellow in need, do so. There is no threat of the king's agents knocking down the door; no fine or tax penalty for failure to help, but an underlying assumption that the one pursuing Living Wisdom will recognize the authority of the Lord over their life and their service to others as accountability to Him.

This passage might reasonably be the basis for Jesus' illustration of the 'needy neighbor' as recorded in Luke 11:5-8. In that parable, the man, warm and safe inside his home, did not want to help, though apparently he had the means to do so. And while to us it does not seem that the man at the door was in truly dire straits, the conventions of hospitality in that culture demanded he provide for this unexpected need.

I'd like to draw attention back to another aspect of Proverbs 3:27. Solomon says that one is not to hold back from giving *"to whom it is due"*. I think this is very important as it tells us that not everyone who comes begging or asking has a right to expect us to meet their needs, nor do we need to be placed under guilt for not helping them. You know as well as I how many scam artists are out there and those for whom a handout is enabling them to continue to live in a sinful way or avoid personal responsibility. Some say help everyone and let the Lord deal with them; give without conditions. I tend to take the perspective that if I suspect the person is playing fast and loose, I am not going to be a party to that.

But for those truly in need, we are responsible to the Lord to minister to them by meeting their needs as we are able. In fact, as we give to those in need, we give to the Lord Himself; so Solomon says:

> "Whoever is generous to the poor lends to [YAHWEH], and he will repay him for his deed...Whoever despises his neighbor is a sinner, but blessed is he who is generous to the poor...Whoever oppresses a poor man insults his Maker, but he who is generous to the needy honors [God]" (19:17; 14:21, 31).

I would further direct our attention to Jesus' teaching in Matthew 25:31-46 in which the kindness shown to the one in need was kindness to the Lord Himself and the refusal to meet the need was in reality a rejection of the Lord.

Living Wisdom causes me to understand that "whoever brings blessing will be enriched, and one who waters will himself be watered" (11:25). I can personally attest to the blessing of giving, whether it is through tithes or other charitable offerings and while the blessing may not necessarily be a material recompense, there is certainly a blessing in the spirit of the follower of Christ.

By contrast, many in our churches cannot understand why they cannot seem to get ahead, why debt piles up, why they put in longer hours and seem to have less at the end of the month. When asked about their obedience to the Lord's teachings to give it is usually revealed that they do not and the truth of the Scripture is proven: "one gives freely, yet grows all the richer; another withholds what he should give, and only suffers want" (11:24).

~The Principle of the Firstfruits

Because all things come from the generous hand of the Lord God, He requires that we acknowledge His beneficence by returning to Him a portion of what we receive in the form of a 'tithe' or 'tenth part'[79]. For Israel the tithe was one tenth of their goods, herds, harvests, etc, which was to be brought to the Tabernacle/Temple either for sacrifice or to be placed in the treasury and to go to the support of the Levitical priests (see Deuteronomy 18:1-8).

The Biblical concept of the tithe finds its origins in the encounter of Abram with Melchizedek in Genesis 14. Upon his return from a successful campaign to rescue his nephew Lot, Abram passed by the city of Salem (Jerusalem). The mysterious priest-king Melchizedek came out to meet Abram, bringing bread and wine. Melchizedek blessed Abram in the Name of "God Most High". In response, Abram gave Melchizedek one tenth of the spoils. The tithe later became part of the

---

[79] I am personally convinced that the tithe should be the minimum standard of Christian giving. If the reader would like a more detailed explanation they may email comfaithnet@gmail.com. A good resource on this topic is *The Tithe: The Minimum Standard for Christian Giving* by George A.E. Salstrand (Baker Book House; Grand Rapids, 1952)

Mosaic Law (Leviticus 27:32; Deuteronomy 14:22).

It is important that we recognize that it is not just how much we are to give to God, but the quality of what we give. Going back to the Law of Moses (e.g. Exodus 34:26), we note that the Israelites were to bring their offering from the firstlings of their flocks and herds and farms in response to how YAHWEH had blessed them. Solomon follows this tradition of the 'firstfruits':

> "Honor [YAHWEH] with your wealth and with the firstfruits of all your produce; then your barns will be filled with plenty, and your vats will be bursting with wine" (3:9-10).

The first part of this passage issues the command to give the *first*fruits. The Hebrew word for this is built on the root *rosh* which has the sense of that which is first or primary; God is worthy to receive the best of all that we have.

This idea of giving the Lord the first and best is found almost at the very beginning of human history. In Genesis 4 we meet two brothers: Cain and Abel. We are told that Abel was a herdsman and Cain was a farmer. The narrative picks up with the brothers preparing to make an offering to YAHWEH: "Cain brought to [YAHWEH] an offering of the fruit of the ground [while] Abel...brought of the firstborn of his flock and of their fat portions" (Genesis 4:3, 4).

God responded to Abel's offering with favor,

but "for Cain and his offering he had no regard" (Genesis 4:5). The reason for God's rejection of Cain's offering has been subject to much discussion. I believe there were three reasons that Cain's offering was inadequate.

First, Abel brought a sacrifice of blood, while Cain did not. Textually, this is the first example of sacrifice made by man to God following the fall of humanity into sin, which is recorded in chapter 3. As that chapter comes to the end, God Himself slays an animal to clothe Adam and Eve in skins (Genesis 3:21). Man sacrificing a blood offering to God is recorded just sentences later.

A second possible reason explaining why God was not pleased with Cain's offering may be found in the 'cursing' of the ground in Genesis 3:17-18. This does not mean that the ground itself is evil or that produce is inferior as God later included offerings of grain as part of the Mosaic sacrificial system (Leviticus 2:1); but perhaps coming so close to this 'curse' we are to recognize the inferiority of Cain's offering.

The third explanation highlights the respective attitudes. It is evident that there is an inferior quality to Cain's heart as well as his offering. Abel, we are told, brought the 'firstlings' (*bekowrah*) of his flocks. These were the best of the best, 'fat portions' of the meatiest and healthiest animals. The Lord later formally staked His claim to the 'fat portions' of the sacrifices (Leviticus 3:16). Cain, in apparent contrast, brought some of his harvest, not necessarily the worst of it, but not the best. We learn, as we follow the account of Cain, that he did not have a heart sensitive to YAHWEH, so this interpretation makes sense. We get the impression that Cain pushed the best off to one side and then half-heartedly selected the best of the rest to bring to the Lord. While each of the three reasons are possible, it is this last, in light of the development of the idea of giving the best to God, that sheds the most light on why God had "no regard" for Cain's offering.

Living Wisdom calls for us to give our best to God — period. Solomon urges his son to follow in this way of Living Wisdom to give God what is of the highest value. While God is worthy to receive our best regardless of what we may get in return, Solomon does show a benefit to the giver. He writes: "...then your barns will be filled with plenty, and your vats will be bursting with wine" (3:10).

Please be very cautious in your understanding and application of this and similar verses. No verse can be taken in isolation from the context and this command, and the promise that comes with it, is part of a wider pattern of Living Wisdom inseparable from several other 'challenge-commands' Solomon puts forward in Proverbs 3 (more on these in chapter 12).

A person cannot ignore God, follow their own ways and then believe that writing a check and calling it a 'tithe' will cover the balance of rejected wisdom. The call to follow God is a call to follow in "all your ways" (3:6) including our wealth and finances. Someone once remarked how we are willing to trust God with our salvation but not with our checkbooks, a comment which cuts closer to home than many people would care to admit.

I would remind you again of the admonition offered at the outset that proverbs are broad principles rather than absolute promises; generally true but not necessarily binding in every situation. The general principle is that when a person is living a wise life before the Lord and when they give to Him gladly from the first and best, not, as Paul will later write, "reluctantly or under compulsion" (2 Corinthians 9:7), that person can expect some form of 'return' from the Lord. In Solomon's time that blessing was an expected agricultural return, grain and new wine being symbolic of God's favor (e.g. Genesis 27:28; Deuteronomy 7:13). While Solomon may have looked for a material return, certainly he understood that there would be an attending spiritual blessing: "A good man obtains favor ['pleasure', 'delight' or 'goodwill'] from [YAHWEH]" (12:2).

Paul expands on this concept for the Church stating that "God is able to make all grace abound to you, so that having all sufficiency in all things at all times, you may abound in every good work" (2 Corinthians 9:8). This tells us that while we *may* receive a material blessing from the Lord ("sufficiency in all things") we *will* certainly gain spiritual reward ("all grace") which will enable us to serve Him more capably.

What can also be stated is that while the one who gives of the first and the best may trust in receiving some type of return, the one who does *not* give or who gives reluctantly of the leftovers should not expect any blessing whatsoever from the Lord. God may choose to offer blessing as a means to gain their attention or draw them closer to Him, but my sense is that this would be a drastic exception rather than the rule.

This is, perhaps, the principle behind such parables as the servants and the talents/minas (Matthew 25; Luke 19) through which Jesus teaches about those who are shown to be faithful in small things being entrusted with greater responsibilities.

One who desires to live a wise life honors the Lord from the first and best of their income and trusts God completely, whether material return follows or not.

*

We have only scratched the surface of what wisdom has to tell us about these matters; much more could certainly be said. I wish for you to take away the following thoughts from our discussion.

First: Living Wisdom has its claim on all things pertaining to our material resources. There is nothing we have that we can withhold from God.

Second: Living Wisdom can help you develop a

new appreciation for your daily work, whether in the marketplace as a homemaker or even in terms of volunteer work. We learn how to pursue our work for God's glory.

Third: Living Wisdom will lead you to a new perspective on giving and the way you use your material resources. All we have comes from God and we must ultimately discover how to use those resources for His service.

Jesus told us that we cannot "serve two masters" (Matthew 6:24). We will either be mastered by materialism or become master of our material.

Be Wise.

Chapter 9

LIVING WISDOM FOR OUR SPIRIT

God has given each person the capacity to connect with Him and He is deeply concerned about whether we avail ourselves of this opportunity or continue to go on living for ourselves. Solomon writes: "all the ways of a man are pure in his own eyes, but [YAHWEH] weighs the spirit" (16:2 literally *spirits* plural). God measures men and women to ascertain whether they have understood their need and turned to Him to fulfill His intended purpose for their lives.

As I mentioned earlier I believe a person is a unity with no division between body, soul and spirit. At the same time I recognize that this unity expresses itself in diversity of function. The body is the physical tool which God created to carry out His will. The soul is the animating power for the body. The spirit is the means through which we connect to God to discover His purposes for us.

Think of it this way. A car is a vessel designed for the purpose of conveying someone from point A to point B, but a car needs something to power it. Fuel is necessary for that car to have the capacity to move. Additionally a car needs a driver to give direction, without which nothing can happen; the car cannot fulfill its purpose.

Applying this admittedly imperfect illustration to a person we would understand the body to be the car itself, the tool; the 'soul' is the fuel, the animating power; the 'spirit' is the driver who gives direction. The system is a unity with diversity. Each needs the other.

In chapter 2 we reflected on the importance of knowing and revering YAHWEH as the source of all wisdom. Here we pick up that theme again by considering more of what Proverbs tells us about how we are to relate to the Lord, the 'driver' of our life, and the blessings of seeking after Him.

~Spiritual Matters Require Spiritual Eyes

All Scripture is inspired by the Spirit of God and as such requires the gift of God's Spirit for discernment and understanding. Proverbs 2:6 makes clear that YAHWEH "gives wisdom; from his mouth come knowledge and understanding." Try as he might, man cannot discover true wisdom in his own power.

One of Job's 'accusers', Elihu, spoke well when he said, "...it is the spirit in man, the breath of the Almighty, that makes him understand" (Job 32:8). One discovers wisdom as they pursue the Lord God; it is He Who "stores up sound wisdom for the upright; he is a shield to those who walk in integrity, guarding the paths of justice and watching over the way of his saints" (2:7-8). The result is the reception of Living Wisdom: "for wisdom will come into your heart, and knowledge will be pleasant to your soul" (2:10).

Perhaps the Apostle Paul had these words in mind as he reasoned with the Corinthians about God's wisdom:

> "No one comprehends the thoughts of God except the Spirit of God. Now we have received not the spirit of the world, but the Spirit who is from God, that we might understand the things freely given us by God. And we impart this in words not taught by human wisdom but taught by the Spirit, interpreting spiritual truths to those who are spiritual" (1 Corinthians 2:11-13).

It is not "the spirit of the world" — the various philosophies and 'isms' concocted by the mind of man—which lead to true knowledge, but the Holy

Spirit. In truth, God *desires* us to know His ways; He does not keep secrets but 'freely gives' us access to His wisdom through the gift of the Holy Spirit. The offer is available to all, but only those who receive God's free gift may gain the spiritual eyes needed to see spiritual truth.

~Feeding the Spirit

Our spiritual aspect requires nourishment no less than our bodies if we are to remain healthy. Living Wisdom impresses upon a person the concern to care for their spirit. Solomon writes: "a joyful heart is good medicine, but a crushed spirit dries up the bones" (17:22). What are the ways by which we may feed and nourish our spirit?

~The Word: God's primary means of communicating with His people has been His Word, whether directly spoken, in its written form or embodied in Jesus. God's Word is precious to the faithful as it is the revelation of His mind and His way.

Proverbs 16:20 says, "...whoever gives thought to the word will discover good, and blessed is he who trusts in [YAHWEH]". While the word *debar* is translated by some as 'a matter' (KJV) or 'instruction' (NIV), I am confident that the author intended to indicate the Word of the Lord. In 16:20 the second phrase (blessing for the one who trusts the Lord) emphasizes the first phrase (discovering good when relying on God's Word)[80].

When God's people take the time to read and consider God's Word good things happen, both as individuals as well as for the believing community. Many statements of faith affirm God's Word as our guide for faith *and* life. Investing the effort in studying and learning how to live out God's Living Wisdom does lead to the discovery of good and leads us to trust our Lord more and more as we realize His way is not just the best way, but is the *only* way.

The Word of God feeds and nourishes our spirit.

~Prayer: If the Word is God's communication to us then prayer is our side of the conversation. While God knows all things, prayer gives us an opportunity to willingly lay our lives open before Him. Prayer helps us to know that God is not distant and unconcerned, but that He "delights in the welfare of his servant[s]" (Psalm 35:27).

Scripture tells us that the Lord "hears the prayer of the righteous" (15:29) and that "[YAHWEH] is near to all who call on him...in truth" (Psalm 145:18). So we recognize that prayer is a means by which we may stay on the path of Living Wisdom.

If we are not living wise lives, we can still pray but likely with a lack of confidence, and rightly so,

---

[80] Many Proverbs are structured in what is called 'parallelism' in which the second phrase relates in some way to the first. Two key types of parallelism in Proverbs are *synonymous*, in which the parts agree, and *antithetic*, in which the parts stand in opposition or contrast. Proverbs 16:20 reflects the synonymous type.

for if sin is not dealt with the Lord can hear but He may not respond (see Psalm 66:18). Confession of sin should be integral to every time of prayer to remove any obstacle that would hinder the fullest connection we can have with our Lord.

In contrast, when we walk in the ways that are pleasing to the Lord we have the confidence that He hears and moves to answer our prayers (Psalm 145:19).

Prayer feeds and nourishes our spirit.

~*Silence & Solitude:* Life is busy; the demands of work and family and other activities, even church related activities, keep us on the go. Someone once called our problem the 'tyranny of the urgent'. One writer picked up this theme in a little pamphlet of the same title. He said, "We live in constant tension between the urgent and the important"[81]. We label as essential too many things which probably aren't as important as we make them out to be.

The concept of silence and solitude is a principle of Living Wisdom. David urges the faithful to take time to be still before the Lord: "ponder in your own hearts on your beds, and be silent" (Psalm 4:4).

Another writes: "Solitude and silence are not self-indulgent exercises [but] are concrete ways of

---

[81] Hummel, Charles E. *Tyranny of the Urgent.* Revised Edition, 1994. www.olemissxa.org. Web. Accessed 10/5/2015. p1

opening to the presence of God beyond human effort and beyond the human constructs that cannot fully contain the divine"[82]. This means that a deliberate cessation of activity is a key means through which we admit our lack of ability to 'manufacture' a relationship with the Lord. We cannot expect to hear the Lord, to spend adequate time in conversation with Him through prayer and the reading of His Word if we are constantly on the go.

Silence & Solitude feed and nourish our spirit.

~*Fellowship in the Faith Community:* Sadly there are times that participating in a local congregation does more to drain the spirit than refresh it. This is not Christ's plan for His Church. Being together with fellow Christians, the camaraderie of God's people is vital to our spiritual health.

I heard a story of a pastor who, one cold afternoon, went to visit an absentee church member. The man welcomed the pastor in, inviting him to join him beside the crackling fire. As he sat down the pastor took the fire poker and gently separated a glowing coal from the fire. He spoke to the man about his need to be a part of the fellowship but the man continually asserted that he was fine on his own and that he didn't need the church. Just before he got up to leave the pastor

---

[82] Barton, Ruth Haley. *Invitation to Solitude and Silence: Experiencing God's Transforming Presence.* InterVarsity Press, Downer's Grove IL, 2010. Print. p31

stooped over and picked up the coal, now black and cold, and placed it in the man's hand. "That, my friend, is what happens to a Christian who does not 'need the church'".

Later in life, Solomon wrote:

> "Two are better than one, because they have a good reward for their toil. For if they fall, one will lift up his fellow. But woe to him who is alone when he falls and has not another to lift him up!" (Ecclesiastes 4:9-10)

We were not designed to be alone as humans even less as Christians. Jesus called *twelve* disciples; He sent them out in pairs; the early Christians gathered *together* for prayer and fellowship.

Left alone, our spirit cools.

Fellowship feeds and nourishes our spirit.

Perhaps you are reading this and realizing that your spirit has been too long undernourished. You've neglected the truly important matters while spending all your time and energy on those things which honestly can wait.

While those methods listed above are important ways for feeding our spirit, all nourishment must begin by knowing Jesus Christ, the source of all sustenance. Apart from Him, everything is an exercise in futility. Our 'religious' activities may ease our mind, but will never truly feed our spirit.

Jesus likened Himself to a life-giving vine which provides nourishment to the branches. These words are perhaps familiar: "I am the vine; you are the branches. Whoever abides in me and I in him, he it is that bears much fruit, for apart from me you can do nothing" (John 15:5).

Living Wisdom calls us to feed our spirit.

~Life after Life

This world is filled with pain and sorrow. In the weeks leading up to this book being finalized for publication, Islamic terrorists attacked Paris killing and wounding scores of people, a man went on a shooting spree in Colorado and fourteen people were gunned down in San Bernardino, California. When we witness such acts, our spirits long for a better world where there is no more suffering.

Living Wisdom is not only the guide for how to live well before the Lord during our time on the earth, but it also brings a person face to face with their mortality causing them to consider their prospects for eternity.

Even under the 'wise' rule of Solomon, the life of the ancient Israelite was not an easy one. Understanding that "man who is born of a woman is few of days and full of trouble" (Job 14:1), God's people learned that they could not depend on the world for their blessings, but needed to look beyond the world to YAHWEH; and rather than look for a life of material ease, they were taught to take pleasure in a growing connection of their spirit to the Lord which would ultimately reach beyond their short life span.

The theological idea of the 'after life', in its infancy in the early part of the Old Testament, can be seen maturing in the wisdom literature. What we observe is the conviction that for God's own people there is an eternal life 'in the land': "the upright will inhabit the land" (2:21), while those who reject the Lord are cast away (2:22).

All of Jewish history, from the ancient to the modern is centered on living in the land which God promised to the patriarchs, Abraham, Isaac and Jacob. The greatest disasters to befall the Jewish people were those periods when they were exiled from the land and their brightest moments were when they took possession of the land.

God promised the land to Abram around 2100BC, but it was not until the days of Joshua, some six hundred years later, that the promise began to be realized. Before they entered Canaan, God warned that if the people failed to keep faith with Him they would be "plucked off the land" (Deuteronomy 28:63) and sent into exile. This tragedy came about in the year 721BC when the northern tribes were conquered by the Assyrian Empire, and in 586BC as the Babylonians overran the southern kingdom. The people found renewed hope and joy when they returned to the land between 538-430BC (the days of Ezra and Nehemiah), but faced catastrophe again when the

Romans cast them out of the land in 70AD and again in 135AD. Except for small scattered pockets, the Jews remained formally alienated from the land until 1948AD when the modern nation of Israel was constituted.

The concept of 'the land' becomes the perfect image for the full and final blessing of YAHWEH, His eternal Kingdom; heaven on earth. To inherit or inhabit this 'land' becomes symbolic of living forever under God's blessing and favor. The word for 'inhabit' in 2:21 is the Hebrew *shakan*; a word that means 'to dwell', often with the implication of a fixed and permanent residence. Another form of this word is *mishkan*, used in reference to the Tabernacle, the place where God would 'dwell' among His people. The point-counterpoint arrangement of 2:21-22 shows us that this permanence is intended. The righteous inhabit in a permanent state while the wicked are taken up and out—also permanently. This is further expressed by the statement: "The righteous will never be removed, but the wicked will not dwell in the land" (10:30).

In the wisdom literature the complete life is life now and life forever. There are many who believe life now is all there is and there are just as many who believe that life now doesn't really matter compared to a life to come. Living Wisdom emphasizes the importance of both as we are moved from life to life: "The path of life leads upward for the prudent, that he may turn away from Sheol beneath" (15:24). Sheol is the name for the place of the dead, translated often as 'the grave'. It is a place of shadow where no activity takes place. It is the destiny of all, for all must die. For "the prudent", the one who has Living Wisdom, Sheol is not the end of the line. God's life-road does not trend downhill, but "upward" that he may turn his back on Sheol, depriving it of its power.

In a wonderful expression of faith which was later applied to the resurrection of Jesus, David exclaimed:

> "For you will not abandon my soul to Sheol, or let your holy one see corruption. You make known to me the path of life; in your presence there is fullness of joy; at your right hand are pleasures forevermore" (Psalm 16:10-11).

David knew that God held the power of life for His people; that the faithful would not be forgotten and abandoned to the grave. David had absolute trust that as one of His favored people, God would "make known...the path of life" which wound its way into the unending delight of His forever presence.

Additionally, Psalm 37 stands out; a song in which David six times calls attention to the hope of God's people to inherit the land "and dwell upon it forever" (Psalm 37:29) while the wicked disappear. It is this Psalm that likely inspired Jesus to utter the now famous words, "Blessed are the meek, for they shall inherit the earth" (Matthew 5:5 compared to Psalm 37:11). Jesus was reiterating the ancient promise of eternal life and connecting Himself with the power of God to grant that life to those who walk in His path. Solomon further declared the hope of the faithful: "In the path of righteousness is life, and in its pathway there is no death" (12:28).

Over two hundred years later, traces of this theme find their way into the words of the prophet Isaiah:

> "And he will swallow up on this mountain the covering that is cast over all peoples, the veil that is spread over all nations. He will swallow up death forever; and [Adonai YAHWEH] will wipe away tears from all faces, and the reproach of his people he will take away from all the earth, for [YAHWEH] has spoken" (Isaiah 25:7-8)

God's way leads to life, both now and for an eternity in which death itself vanishes.

*

If we are to live well before the Lord, we must put ourselves in position to commune and communicate with Him. If our spiritual lives are not tended, they will grow dry and cold; we will wonder why we don't seem to hear from God and become discouraged in our Christian walk. Living

Wisdom, the skilled driver of our lives, points us to the path of spiritual health, preparing us for a life well lived now and giving us the hope for a future life stretching on into the brightness of an endless day.

Be Wise.

Chapter 10

WALKING IN LIVING WISDOM

Having come to a new or renewed sense of the importance of seeking God's Living Wisdom, the next matter at hand is how we go about putting it into practice. There is no literal signpost which says 'good way', so how is the wise person to live before the Lord and demonstrate growth in wisdom?

~Living Wisely before the Lord

Proverbs 4:20-27 offers some practical insight, a 'five step guide' if you will, for living well and wisely; broad principles which may serve as an effective guide to wise walking.

~Learn and Remember Truth

The first step in walking wisdom's road is to listen carefully with the desire to develop a good memory: "My son, be attentive to my words; incline your ear to my sayings. Let them not escape from your sight; keep them within your heart. For they are life to those who find them…" (4:20-22).

When we read about the lives of the patriarchs and early leaders of Israel, we note how often they set up altars and memorial monuments[83]. This was done as a means of remembering what God had accomplished for them. By contrast the terrible days of the Judges came about because the people forgot (see Judges 2:10-11).

In the Church, we have children and new believers begin by learning the foundational accounts[84] of the Bible because they are simple to remember and their teaching is easily recalled. It is vital to the development of Living Wisdom that we not only learn, but remember.

~Internalize and Practice Truth

While memorizing the popular 'stories' of the Bible is a good start, much more is needed to discover and practice Living Wisdom. The second

---

[83] For some examples consider Jacob's pillar at Bethel (Genesis 28 & 35); Moses' memorial (Exodus 24) and Joshua's stones from the Jordan River (Joshua 4).

[84] The Bible is historical in nature and not a collection of fictional tales or myth and thus we need to be cautious when using the word 'story' as it relates to the accounts of the Bible. We are dealing with 'Thus says the Lord' and not 'Once upon a time.'

step in travelling wisdom's way is to make the truth of God's teaching a very part of who we are: "Keep your heart with all vigilance, for from it flow the springs of life" (4:23).

Jesus will later say that "what comes out of the mouth proceeds from the heart" (Matthew 15:18), meaning that what dominates the heart is what dominates the person. If goodness and righteousness are in control, a person will be good and righteous, whereas if evil runs the show, evil will flow.

The Psalmist was right to encourage us to 'hide God's Word in our hearts' (Psalm 119:11). It is nowhere near enough to give mere verbal or intellectual assent to God's ways. His truth must inform and impact every aspect of who we are and what we do. We must keep watch daily, continually asking, 'what dominates my heart?'[85]

~Speak What Suits the Truth

Just as Jesus said that what is in a man's heart will show forth in his life, so we take the third step in walking wisdom's way: keeping close watch on our mouth: "Put away from you crooked speech, and put devious talk far from you" (4:24).

Solomon uses two words, each carrying the idea of something distorted. The first word, translated in the ESV as 'crooked' is *ikkesh* which designates something that is twisted, usually as a result of sin.

---

[85] Wiersbe, Warren W. *The Bible Exposition Commentary: Wisdom and Poetry.* Victor; 2004 Electronic Database; Biblesoft Inc.

The word rendered 'devious' is *looz*, which also speaks of deviancy. In both cases the reader of Proverbs is warned to keep watch over their words, to refuse to speak anything that is untrue or 'twisted'. I suppose that this would include even those 'little white lies' which we are told do no harm.

These 'crooked' words are not limited to lies but include cruel, hurtful and abusive words as well. How many of us are prone to let our agitation spill out in words that are not always edifying? Words that tear down do not reflect God's heart and are to be avoided at all costs.

How can we claim to have wisdom if we cannot control what comes out of our mouths? How can we claim to be led by God's Spirit if the evidence reveals a different 'master' ruling in our hearts? Wisdom's path requires a commitment to speaking in ways that honor wisdom's Source.

~See What Honors the Truth

Step four in journeying down the road of wisdom is to be diligent towards what comes before our eyes: "Let your eyes look directly forward, and your gaze be straight before you" (4:25).

Following the previous idea of perversity this proverb has to do with the need to keep our eyes from wandering towards enticements which may harm and destroy us. This includes not only lewd images or things of a 'pornographic' nature, but also those things which might lead to other sin such as covetousness or jealousy or anger.

What we see goes into our hearts and minds. The good, like fresh air and sweet water, brings refreshment to our spirits while the evil festers and, if not rooted out, reveals itself in ugly ways. We are warned to keep our eyes fixed on those things which are good and pure.

The applications are broad: husbands keep your eyes on your wife; businessmen keep your eyes on your integrity; rulers keep your eyes on truth and justice. Keep your eyes on that which befits wisdom and the One Who is her Source.

~Measure Your Life According to the Truth

The fifth and final step in walking the path of wisdom is to regularly evaluate your progress: "Ponder the path of your feet; then all your ways will be sure. Do not swerve to the right or to the left; turn your foot away from evil" (4:26-27).

The walk of faith is a journey, the end of which none of us reach until Christ establishes His perfect and eternal Kingdom. Therefore, as we measure our progress, we cannot on the one hand become overly pleased with what we perceive to be advancement, nor can we allow ourselves to become overly dismayed or discouraged at what seems to be slow development. Keep perspective!

I have heard that the best method farmers use to plow a straight path is to fix their eyes on a point in the distance and keep the plow pointed in that direction. But it makes sense that they would also scan the ground in front of them for stones or other obstacles which would hinder their progress.

So it is with this walk down wisdom's path. As we fix our eyes on the goal (Jesus Himself according to Hebrews 12:1-2) we should scan the ground in front of us for those 'small things' that trip us up such as pride, anger, frustration, greed or bitterness, none of which by itself can derail us completely, but all of which can knock us off our feet for a spell. Keep your eyes on the goal and know the ground.

I pray the Lord uses these principles to guide and protect you as you move down the path of Living Wisdom.

~Markers of Growth

As we grow, our character and the corresponding actions will begin to reflect new priorities which are contrary to the wisdom of the world but demonstrate increasing maturity. As we develop, we can expect certain qualities to emerge naturally.

~A wise person is truly humble before the Lord.

We spoke of pride earlier, and here we consider the other end of that spectrum. To be humble is to have a right estimation of yourself and your position before God. To be humble is to know that He is the Creator and you are the creature—a highly valued and loved creature—but a creature nonetheless, with the limitations and weaknesses that go along with 'creatureliness'. Humility knows that apart from the life-giving, life-sustaining power of the Lord we are nothing.

Living Wisdom leads us to this understanding and in return we find the blessing of God: "Toward the scorners [YAHWEH] is scornful, but to the humble he gives favor" (3:34).

To the one who places themselves in correct position to the Lord, He grants His mercy and His kindness. He lifts up the 'lowly' and grants them a place of honor (see 29:23). He rewards the humble with spiritual blessing and life (22:4).

We will see growth in Living Wisdom as we push aside pride and humble ourselves before the Lord.

~A wise person develops an aversion to sin, actively fighting against it.

Living Wisdom begins with reverence for the Lord. Reverence for the Lord leads to "hatred of evil" (8:13). Therefore Living Wisdom by its very nature pushes against sin, seeking to purge it from our lives. It is not an automatic victory, as you are well aware; we must be ready to actively engage in the battle every moment, every day. This may seem daunting, but as we draw closer to the Lord and seek His ways the challenge becomes less ominous. And while we can never let our guard down we do find that sin becomes more of an annoyance, like a pesky fly, rather than an exhaustingly constant crisis.

It *is* possible to turn from sin! Wisdom tells us: "By steadfast love and faithfulness iniquity is atoned for, and by the fear of [YAHWEH] one turns away from evil" (16:6). When I know my sin is paid for through God's mercy and love and I give Him the honor and respect He is due, I *can* turn away from sin. And when you turn your back on something it loses a whole lot of power. We are told to walk away from bullies. Why? Because when you walk away you remove the threat and power. The bully is still there, but somehow diminished. Every time you are faced with sin and in the Name of the Lord you turn and walk away from it, it loses a little bit more power.

Provided we remain in our relationship with the Lord and "continue in the fear of [YAHWEH] all the day" (23:17) sin soon has little ability to grip us at all.

We will see growth in Living Wisdom as we learn to successfully fight against sin in our lives.

~ A wise person develops a deep sense for justice.

The heart of God is for the poor and the downtrodden of the world. He knows that the tendency of fallen man is to oppress and exploit others, seeking to attain worldly wealth and power at their expense.

The Lord built provisions into the legal code of Israel for the care of the widow, the orphan and the poor of the land to prevent exploitation among His chosen community[86]. Early in the Hebrew settlement of Canaan there seemed to be equality among the people, but by Solomon's time there were definite distinctions between the rich and the poor and the problems that went with such inequality.

Because those in need are dear to God's heart, they should be so to God's people. Proverbs is replete with calls to aid the poor and warnings against oppression. Solomon reminds his son that the fear of YAHWEH is the key for him to "understand righteousness and justice and equity, every good path" (2:9). When a person is seeking the Lord, they will begin to desire those things that matter to Him.

Living Wisdom calls out for God's people to "do righteousness and justice" which is "more acceptable to [YAHWEH] than sacrifice" (21:3). Righteousness and justice do not take place by putting a 'sacrifice' of money into an offering basket, but in acts of daily living in which we care for those in need, having a heart sensitive to opportunities for service and compassion.

We will see growth in Living Wisdom as we learn to love those things which matter most to God.

---

[86] Exodus 22:21-27 offers a comprehensive example of this law.

~A wise person exhibits a devotion to the Word of God.

The practical application of most every sermon or teaching I give for accomplishing growth in our spiritual life can be boiled down into two activities: prayer and reading the Bible. Fellowship with God through such spiritual disciplines is essential to Living Wisdom.

When Solomon completed the building of the Temple he offered a prayer of dedication and then a benediction for the people. At the conclusion of that blessing he said: "Let your heart therefore be wholly true to [YAHWEH] our God, walking in his statutes and keeping his commandments, as at this day" (1 Kings 8:61).

Solomon understood the need to remain in fellowship with the Lord through obedience to His Word. He recognized that to ignore or reject the Word of God was a recipe for disaster: "Whoever despises the word brings destruction on himself" (13:13) and "if one turns away his ear from hearing the law, even his prayer is an abomination" (28:9), but "whoever gives thought to the word will discover good, and blessed is he who trusts in [YAHWEH]" (16:20).

Like one's relationship to their spouse, a relationship with God is, of necessity, a whole hearted endeavor. Sadly, 'wise' Solomon allowed his relationship to be compromised and he fell into a half-hearted condition towards God, forgetting the Word which caused him to be led into idol worship (1 Kings 11:1-8).

We will see growth in Living Wisdom as we devote ourselves to the Word of God.

Living well before the Lord takes effort, dedication and determination to develop a heart that beats in time with His. It is work, but the resulting life of Wisdom will more than repay the effort.

~Other Expressions of Living Wisdom (Proverbs 30-31)

At the end of the book of Proverbs (chapters 30-31) we find two additional sections from the hand of otherwise unknown writers, Agur and Lemuel. Who are these men and why are their words included in the book?

The name *Agur* means 'stranger' or 'gathered together'[87] while *Lemuel* means 'God with him'[88] or 'belonging to God'[89]. The rabbis identify him with Solomon but this cannot be known for certain.

A possibility for the identity of these two men comes from the word *massa* which is translated in 30:1 & 31:1 as 'oracle'. The word could indicate the prophetic nature of the sayings of these writers, yet

---

[87] Hitchcock, Rev. Roswell D., *Hitchcock's New and Complete Analysis of the Holy Bible.* A.J. Johnson: New York, 1871. Print. p1104

[88] Ibid p1109

[89] Bromiley, Geoffrey W. (Editor), *International Standard Bible Encyclopedia*, revised edition, Copyright © 1979 by Wm. B. Eerdmans Publishing Co. Electronic Database: Biblesoft Inc.

as the International Standard Bible Encyclopedia comments, the term "usually conveys the sense of doom or judgment, which does not fit the context [of Proverbs 30-31]"[90]. Another possibility is that *massa* might be a reference to their home in a region in Arabia settled by one of the sons of Ishmael. This would make these men of Arab, not Jewish, descent.

This second option may receive further credence based on the sudden disappearance of the Name YAHWEH. Of the 88 times the Name is used in Proverbs, only two come in 30-31. It is reasonably possible that Agur and Lemuel were Arab sages not directly associated with the Covenant God, but were moved to record Living Wisdom beyond the borders of Solomon's kingdom.

What we learn from this is that whether Jew or Gentile, male or female, king or commoner, Living Wisdom is truly universal for any who seek YAHWEH, God of Israel.

Let's examine some of what they have to say noting that while the principles overlap with point of previous discussion, they bear repeating.

~Agur

Agur begins by chastising himself for his limited grasp of wisdom because he has failed to know God: "Surely I am too stupid to be a man. I have

---

[90] Ibid

not the understanding of a man. I have not learned wisdom, nor have I knowledge of the Holy One" (30:2-3). As wisdom begins with knowing the Lord, it should be of no surprise to us that Agur connects his lack of wisdom to his lack of relationship to God.

Agur's questions are designed to demonstrate, like the questions contained in Job 38-39, that there are matters which are beyond the reach of human comprehension. However, there are other matters which man in fact can grasp and therefore he bears a responsibility to act accordingly, as Moses related to Israel: "The secret things belong to [YAHWEH] our God, but the things that are revealed belong to us and to our children forever, *that we may do* all the words of this law" (Deuteronomy 29:29 my emphasis)

Agur confessed that "every word of God proves true; he is a shield to those who take refuge in him" (30:5) and warns his hearers: "Do not add to his words, lest he rebuke you and you be found a liar" (30:6). In other words, Living Wisdom begins in the Word of God, and man should never presume to know more than God.

Living Wisdom, for Agur, is manifested in different ways.

~*Contentment:* A wise person seeks that which is needed for the day, putting their hope and trust in God for His provision:

"...give me neither poverty nor riches;

feed me with the food that is needful for me, lest I be full and deny you and say, 'Who is [YAHWEH]?' or lest I be poor and steal and profane the name of my God" (30:7-9).

Agur recognized the pitfalls of wealth in leading his heart away from God and the downfall of poverty, leading a person to compromise their integrity. He prayed for his needs and a spirit of contentment in God.

~Respect: A wise person develops healthy relationships and treats others with decency and respect. Agur makes the point using negative examples: "Do not slander a servant to his master, lest he curse you and you be held guilty. There are those who curse their fathers and do not bless their mothers" (3:10-11).

These are qualities of fools who are morally and spiritually bankrupt, destined for destruction at the hands of God. Honor and respect for others mark a person of Living Wisdom.

~Humility: A wise person understands their place before God. Again using negative language, Agur points to the way of a wise life: "There are those who are clean in their own eyes but are not washed of their filth. There are those—how lofty are their eyes, how high their eyelids lift!" (30:12-13).

We have already considered the destructive influence of pride. Arrogant and prideful people cannot see the mess of their own lives. They are so busy sniffing the air with upturned nose they don't see the mire they wallow in. People with a prideful spirit cannot be wise. The humble find the way of Living Wisdom.

~*Compassion:* Wise people serve others; fools use others for their own gain. Wise people build up; fools destroy: "There are those whose teeth are swords, whose fangs are knives, to devour the poor from off the earth, the needy from among mankind" (30:14).

People with Living Wisdom see suffering and it breaks their hearts. They want to know what they can do to help. Fools see suffering and seek how to use it to their advantage, actively working to destroy the weak and helpless.

Agur continues his evaluation of wisdom in several illustrations from the world around him (30:15-29). At the end he sums up his discovery: "If you have been foolish, exalting yourself, or if you have been devising evil, put your hand on your mouth. For pressing milk produces curds, pressing the nose produces blood, and pressing anger produces strife" (30:32-33).

This is a warning for us to consider our ways. Have you been displaying behaviors that demonstrate a complete lack of Living Wisdom? The time has come for you to sit down and be quiet. If you don't, you will find the end to be most unpleasant.

Agur teaches us that Living Wisdom changes

our attitudes.

~Lemuel

King Lemuel learned wisdom from his mother (31:1) recalling the importance of those intergenerational relationships considered earlier.

Lemuel's mother begins with a thrice repeated question: "what are you doing?" (31:2) His mother, perhaps observing her son's behavior, finally catches him by the arm and challenges him. 'Son...what are you thinking!?' In her advice she teaches us all Living Wisdom.

~*Marital Fidelity:* It was common practice for kings to keep a harem, women in addition to his wife to 'serve his needs'. Lemuel's mother cautions him: "do not give your strength to women, your ways to those who destroy kings" (31:3). If managing a household with one husband and one wife is hard enough, imagine trying to manage a kingdom with the competing interests of multiple wives; sapping the strength of the king and causing the destruction of kingdoms. By way of example, the Bible records Solomon's record setting collection of 700 wives and 300 mistresses who "turned away his heart" from following devotedly after YAHWEH (1 Kings 11:3). This ended in the ruin of the kingdom.

I'm not a king, but I have a duty to uphold the pledge I made to my wife to 'forsake all others'. Husbands and wives are bound to fidelity to their marriage partner. Keeping our homes intact is hard enough without adding the destructive nature of extramarital affairs.

What of those who are single? If you plan to marry someday, pledge your faithfulness to that person, even if you have not met them yet! If you do not plan to marry, as a Christian you have joined yourself to Christ and owe Him ultimate faithfulness.

People of Living Wisdom are faithful to their one spouse.

~*Self-Control/Sobriety:* We have already discussed the destructive nature of alcohol abuse. That theme is picked up here.

> "It is not for kings, O Lemuel, it is not for kings to drink wine, or for rulers to take strong drink, lest they drink and forget what has been decreed and pervert the rights of all the afflicted" (31:4-5).

Lemuel is a king with responsibilities for the well-being of his kingdom. Can that be accomplished if he is consumed by drink? Drunken kings do not serve their subjects well and find their kingdoms taken from them (see 1 Kings 16:9). This is what his mother warns him against.

I'm not a king, but I have responsibilities in my ministry and in my household. I have stated my position that the overall teaching of the Scripture does not forbid the use of alcohol, but rather the drinking to excess and drunkenness. If I am pursuing the 'pleasures' of alcohol I will be unable to devote myself to those responsibilities.

People of Living Wisdom pursue sobriety and self control.

~*Compassion and Justice:* Kings had a responsibility to all their subjects, especially the poor and helpless. A wise king protected the vulnerable from exploitation and distress.

Lemuel's mother said: "Give strong drink to the one who is perishing, and wine to those in bitter distress; let them drink and forget their poverty and remember their misery no more" (31:6-7).

That advice seems strange doesn't it? At first glance it appears that the king is to get poor people drunk so they forget their situation. Not so. The very poor in that culture had little hope, joy or comfort and while the king could not always lift them out of poverty or hardship, he could provide opportunities for the people to gather and enjoy life, taking their minds off their problems.

Lemuel's mother continues: "Open your mouth for the mute, for the rights of all who are destitute. Open your mouth, judge righteously, defend the rights of the poor and needy" (31:8-9).

The king had a duty to advocate for the poor. If they owed money, he would ensure they weren't being extorted for interest or forced into slavery. If they had a bad crop due to drought or pestilence, he could step in and prevent their lands from being seized by investors.

I am not a king, but there are those in need all

around me. I can do something to help the poor and helpless. I can invite a needy neighbor to dinner and help them find enjoyment for the moment even if I cannot change their life. I can keep alert for needs of justice in my community, maybe joining an advocacy group.

People of Living Wisdom have deep concern for the situation of those in need.

Lemuel teaches us that Living Wisdom changes our behavior.

~The Virtuous Woman

The book of Proverbs concludes with a poem to a wise and virtuous woman. The poem celebrates the qualities of wisdom which, while displayed through an anonymous woman, can be developed in anyone.

~The wise person is trustworthy: The wise woman is highly valued by her husband because he knows she can be counted on to do well: "The heart of her husband trusts in her, and he will have no lack of gain. She does him good, and not harm, all the days of her life" (31:11-12).

Since the wife in Israelite culture held such an important role in the ordering and overseeing of household and business affairs, one who was flighty, unskilled or lacking integrity could be a disaster to not only the individual home, but to the stability of the community network.

Living Wisdom people carry out the responsibilities given them with skill and efficiency, garnering the trust and respect of those around them.

~The wise person is industrious: This woman demonstrates an amazing knack for managing and supporting her household: "She seeks wool and flax, and works with willing hands" (31:13); "She considers a field and buys it..." (31:16); "She makes linen garments and sells them; she delivers sashes to the merchant" (31:24).

She engages in a variety of enterprises and works hard to see that each succeeds. She does not fear failure because she trusts her good judgment and her ability.

Living Wisdom people consider what they need to do and then do it to the absolute best of their ability. They are willing to explore a variety of opportunities.

~The wise person is generous: The wise woman knows that not all are as fortunate as she and she stands ready to help: "She opens her hand to the poor and reaches out her hands to the needy" (31:20).

Not everyone is in a position to manage a family; not skilled to be an artisan; do not have the capital to begin a start up business. The woman knows that many fall through the cracks and extends some of her profit to alleviate their hardship.

Living Wisdom people are generous and compassionate to those who are in need.

~*The wise person is forward thinking:* The wise woman can see the path of life; she knows what is coming and prepares for it: "She is not afraid of snow...for all her household are clothed in scarlet. She makes bed coverings for herself...she laughs at the time to come" (31:21-22, 25).

While it is summer, she prepares what her family will need for winter. She is confident to meet the challenges ahead because they do not take her by surprise. When they come, she laughs at their feeble attempts to overtake her.

Living Wisdom people look ahead at what is likely to come about and then make appropriate plans. They do not wait for difficult times before making a plan, but have already dealt with the challenge before it appears.

~*The wise person seeks to bring honor to those around them:* The wise woman has acted in such honorable ways that those associated with her are honored: "Her husband is known in the gates when he sits among the elders of the land" (31:23).

The gate was the most important place in the town. It was where the elders met to discuss the governing of the community, where they convened the court and judged legal cases. It was where business was transacted. It was where news of the village and of the outside world was broadcast. When the husband of the wise woman comes to the gate, he is given additional respect and honor because of the reputation of his wife.

Living Wisdom people desire to have such a good reputation that those associated with them may also gain favor.

The virtuous woman teaches us that Living Wisdom makes us stronger, healthier more effective people.

*

From kings to commoners; men and women of any background can lay hold of Living Wisdom. We discover that walking in wisdom is a reward in itself allowing us to discover a life well lived before the Lord. By witnessing the lives and listening to the words of those who have gone before us on the path of Living Wisdom, we are given principles by which to successfully live well before the Lord. These faithful people are the signposts pointing us to wisdom's road.

Be Wise.

Chapter 11

THE COST OF REJECTING
LIVING WISDOM

Throughout the book we have been reflecting on the importance of seeking the Lord, noting the blessings attending that search.   It makes sense therefore that there will be consequences for failing to seek God and for rejecting His Living Wisdom. It falls to us now to consider those consequences.

~Wisdom Ignored- A Case Study

Proverbs is addressed to Solomon's son, but considering his many wives and concubines, Solomon must have fathered many sons. In many ways, Proverbs is a primer for a king and so seems logical that it is the heir to the throne who most needed to hear wisdom's call. Alas, the record shows this particular son, Rehoboam, failed to heed the lessons his father sought to impart. Rehoboam's life and rule demonstrate the severity of the consequences that may arise when wisdom is ignored.

Solomon himself had failed to keep the principles of Living Wisdom by failing to guard his heart, weakening in his commitment to fear and honor YAHWEH, and falling tragically into idol worship (1 Kings 11:3-8). As a consequence, God determined that the kingdom would be divided, with the ten northern tribes being given over to Jeroboam (1 Kings 11:26ff.). Reading the text 'after-the-fact', we know this purpose of the Lord (1 Kings 11:31), but as these things were unfolding, Rehoboam had no knowledge of this plan. What happened next was completely in his hands.

After Solomon's death, Jeroboam returned from his exile in Egypt and challenged Rehoboam: "Your father made our yoke heavy. Now therefore lighten the hard service of your father and his heavy yoke on us, and we will serve you." (1 Kings 12:4)

Rehoboam stood at a crossroads: here was his opportunity to keep the nation united under the banner of the House of David or cause it to fragment. To aid him in his decision, Rehoboam sought the advice of two groups of counselors.

We considered the importance of choosing positive voices to guide us in wisdom and thought through the danger of negative influences which tend to lead us astray. Both aspects are on display here.

He first looked to the older men who had advised his father. These men understood the delicate nature of the situation and urged a relaxation of Solomon' policies through which the people had become embittered (1 Kings 12:6-7). Then, the new king sought direction from the younger men, those with whom he had grown up. This younger group, possibly excited by their new authority, incited Rehoboam to flex his muscles and establish his rule by a show of force and cruelty (1 Kings 12:8-11).

Scripture tells us that Rehoboam "abandoned the counsel that the old men gave him" (1 Kings 12:8). He chose to turn his back on wisdom and listen instead to the wrong voices. As a result those northern brethren 'abandoned' Rehoboam beginning an on-and-off-again civil war which would cover the next 250 years. Under the rule of Rehoboam, the people of the south became spiritually weak and morally corrupt, acting out the grossest sin and idolatry (1 Kings 14:22-24), finally bowing in defeat to an Egyptian army (1 Kings 14:25-28).

How could Rehoboam act so foolishly in the face of the overwhelming wisdom passed down by his father? Part of the answer certainly must lie in Solomon's own failures. For all his wisdom perhaps it was Solomon's *actions* which made the greater impression upon his son rather than his words.

In his book *Kingdom of Priests*, Eugene Merrill reflects that Solomon's sin did not invalidate his possession of wisdom, but rather revealed his failure to consistently order his life and household by the principles of wisdom[91]. He comments, "...we must simply make the point that it is possible to be wise in the biblical sense of the term and yet fail to live out the implications of that wisdom."[92]

Knowing what to do and actually doing it are different issues altogether. This inconsistency still plagues us today, doesn't it? We often know what we are supposed to do to live in ways which lead to greater health and happiness in the Lord, but are either unable or unwilling to put these ways into practice on a consistent basis. We are left with half a kingdom, so to speak, in a state of civil war between our spirit and our flesh (see Galatians 5:15).

~Know Thyself

A cunning enemy does not attack strong points but probes for weaknesses in the opposing defenses. It is a person growing in Living Wisdom who takes an accounting of themselves, to understand their mind and heart, what drives them

[91] Merrill p313
[92] Ibid p312

and what their own weaknesses are. A person who cannot be enticed into sin through alcohol may be tripped up by anger. One who is sexually pure may be caught by gossip.

Those who are following the Lord and growing in wisdom are learning how to not *intentionally* wander into sinful ways. They are discovering those subtle habits or attitudes which, if unchecked, lead away from the path of Living Wisdom.

Solomon offers a list we would do well to pay close attention to. While we have thought about several of these already, I have no problem revisiting them in order that we not remain unaware of the traps which our enemy lays for us (see 2 Corinthians 2:11).

> "There are six things that [YAHWEH] hates, seven that are an abomination to him: haughty eyes, a lying tongue, and hands that shed innocent blood, a heart that devises wicked plans, feet that make haste to run to evil, a false witness who breathes out lies, and one who sows discord among brothers" (6:16-19)

For many it may be hard to grasp that God can 'hate' something. The word *sanay* is a word which "...expresses an emotional attitude toward persons and things which are opposed, detested, despised and with which one wishes to have no contact or relationship."[93]

Yes, God does 'hate'. He opposes, detests and despises sin and will tolerate no contact with it whatsoever. One of the more stunning truths of Jesus' sacrifice is that the sinless Son of God became sin for us (see 2 Corinthians 5:21) and when this happened God the Father hid His Face, not being willing to look upon His Son[94].

Of all sin, perhaps it is idolatry that God detests most. Scripture uses the word *tow'ebah* (translated 'abomination') to refer to the worship of idols which is 'abominable' to the Holy God.

Because all idolatry finds its way back to the 'godhood of the self', Proverbs 6 lists seven 'abominations' which refer not to statues of wood or stone, but to people. Seven traps, various sins of the eyes, mouth, hands, heart and feet which, if we do not remain alert to the enemy's schemes, can seriously hamper our discovery and practice of Living Wisdom.

~Trap #1- "haughty eyes": This is pride, and it is no surprise that it sits at the top of the list. The phrase is indicative of a conceit which elevates a person above others for any possible reason: the car they drive, the house they live in, the success of their kids on the dean's list. You can recognize this trap when you cannot be happy for another

---

[93] Harris, Archer, and Waltke p880

[94] Consider Habakkuk 1:13 (NIV) and Isaiah 54:7-8 with the significance of Jesus' cry of forsakenness on the cross and the darkness which came over the land upon His death.

person's success or you cannot let them speak of a success without 'one-upping' them; tipping the scales in your favor. Haughty eyes are in direct contrast to a spirit of love for and service to others.

~Trap #2- *"a lying tongue"*: This is a spirit of deception, often done purely out of self interest. Sometimes we lie to spare someone's feelings and justify it by saying we are being 'tactful'. Sometimes we lie to save ourselves embarrassment or to get out of a minor inconvenience. Regardless of the reasons, a lying tongue is contradictory to a profession of faith in a perfectly true God.

~Trap #3- *"hands that shed innocent blood"*: Immediately we think of violence, but seeing as how the overwhelming majority of you reading have never literally killed anyone, we should seek another application. If we think of this 'trap' in a non-lethal/non-violent context perhaps we might think of unjustified anger, which Jesus says is just as wicked as murder (Matthew 5:21-22) or perhaps betrayal, which is turning against someone with selfish intent. Are these not ways in which we might 'shed innocent blood'? The blameless have a strong protector in YAHWEH (10:29) and He will defend them. We must take great care that we do not injure others in these more subtle but no less destructive ways.

~Trap #4- *"a heart that devises wicked plans"*: Our instincts may again lead us to think of 'really bad people' who plot to defraud the elderly, blow up buildings or attack policemen in the street, but we must again bring it to a common level. This is a description of any unrighteous motives we may have. The roots of this issue are jealousy, envy and covetousness. We want something that we perhaps should not or cannot have, so we devise schemes to get what we want and then fabricate logical and moral loopholes to escape the guilt; manipulating events to ensure that we get our own way. This is the spirit behind buying an expensive dress or jacket for a special occasion and then returning it after the event and getting a refund. It is why elections are rigged and bribes are offered. Our God is righteous in all His ways; His people are to be as well.

~*Trap #5*- *"feet that make haste to run to evil"*: I see in this a spirit of rashness. Our desire again is to make this so extreme that it doesn't apply personally. We might consider this to be the quality of a person who robs a bank or hijacks a plane. But what if it applies to a person who cannot control their temper or acts impulsively without thinking of the consequences? That makes it a bit more personal doesn't it? Rather than rush to evil, Peter tells Christians that they must "turn away from evil and do good...seek peace and pursue it" (1 Peter 3:11).

~*Trap #6*- *"a false witness who breathes out lies"*: Breathing is involuntary; something that comes naturally to us without thinking. This then is a description of a person who's 'lying tongue' has become so habitual that they don't even stop to think about truth; in fact, whatever serves them in that moment is 'truth'. This is also the spirit of gossip mentioned earlier. Do you know someone for whom the lies and deception have become so 'natural' that you expect nothing they say to be the truth? It is scary. In Revelation 19:11 the glorious Jesus is named "Faithful and True". May it be that His people emulate Him in this!

~Trap #7- "one who sows discord among brothers": Throughout the Scripture we read accounts of division and the chaos it causes: Adam and Eve (Genesis 3); Rachel and Leah (Genesis 29-30); Saul and David (1 Samuel 18-27); Euodia and Syntyche (Philippians 4:2). Sadly the spirit of contentiousness and divisiveness affects many brothers and sisters in many different churches. Everyone wants their way and no one wants to serve; so there is backbiting, more gossip, more lies. Local churches have endured splits and many have closed their doors forever because certain people seek to divide.

The Apostle John wrote of a man named Diotrephes "who likes to put himself first [and] does not acknowledge our authority" (3 John 9). Diotrephes was more intent on keeping the church divided rather than doing what would bring unity. Such a spirit is abhorrent to the Lord Who prizes unity.

The Word tells us, "...how good and pleasant it is when brothers live together in unity!" (Psalm 133:1). In fact, unity among the people of God is so important that Jesus told His disciples it would be a key indicator that He was truly sent by the Father: "May they be brought to complete unity to let the world know that you sent me and have loved them even as you have loved me" (John 17:23). Unity in the Church is serious business and that which threatens unity is an abomination to the Lord.

The enemy lays these traps with the intent to pull us off the path of Living Wisdom and seriously hamper our ability to connect with God and with our fellow believers in healthy ways. Every one of us needs to take the time to learn what causes us to stumble so that when the attack comes we will be able to withstand it. As Christians, we have the advantage. The Holy Spirit leads us to a "godly grief [which] produces a repentance that leads to salvation" (2 Corinthians 7:10); we 'plead the cross', trusting the blood of Jesus for our forgiveness and are set free knowing our sin does not lead to rejection of God's Wisdom resulting in condemnation.

~Future Consequences

The internal conflict and inconsistent living which results from ignoring wisdom is problematic for the present moment, but greater consequences for the future exist if the issues are not remedied. I commented in chapter 9 that Living Wisdom 'brings a person face to face with their mortality and the prospects for their eternity'. There are wonderful promises for those who find wisdom, but a severe and tragic end awaiting those who reject God's Living Wisdom.

As mentioned, the theological idea of the 'after life' is developing within the wisdom literature. I detailed the blessing of that future life as the faithful "inhabit the land" (2:21). There is a second side to that passage as Solomon declares that the wicked will be "cut off" and "rooted out" (2:22). Recalling that the 'land' is a representation for the final and perfect Kingdom of God, it becomes clear that the wicked can never hope to be found there.

As we consider the consequences of rejecting God's Living Wisdom, I feel the following principle to be essential: Unless Scripture leads us to understand an image as symbolic or figurative, we should take the author's most literal meaning[95].

I have written elsewhere:

> "We must agree at the outset that for language to have any value, words must mean what they mean in their plain sense...to change the meaning of...words without cause is unwarranted and

---

[95] When we read in Revelation of a 'beast' rising from the sea, we know that we are to take this as symbolic because in Daniel 'beasts' have been interpreted to mean worldly governments or empires. However when John states that he saw an 'angel' we are to take this as some form of literal heavenly being.

indefensible."[96]

The various word images associated with the punishment of those who reject God all have the same theme: the ultimate consequence for those who reject YAHWEH (classified as 'the wicked') will be the complete and irreversible loss of life and hope[97].

The plain meaning of the two words used in Proverbs 2:22 leave little to question. The word for 'cut off' is *carath*, a word meaning 'to divide and remove'. It was a key part of ancient covenants; to 'cut a covenant' involved the sacrifice of animals and dividing them in halves, such as is seen in God's covenant with Abram in Genesis 15 (verses 7-11 specifically). To be 'cut off' and forever excluded from Israel was the consequence for those who failed to keep the covenant of circumcision (Genesis 17:14) or who consumed leaven during the festival of unleavened bread (Exodus 12:19). The other word, translated 'rooted out', is *nasach*. To

---

[96] Fernald, Chad C. A Theology of Hope over a Theology of Horror. Blog Post: comfaithnet.blogspot.com. Blogger.com. Feb-Mar 2015. Web.

[97] I am convinced that the Scriptures do not teach an eternity of torment for those apart from God's salvation but rather that these will be judged by God and cast into a place the book of Revelation calls the Lake of Fire where they will, in God's timing, be finally and fully destroyed, ceasing to exist. This view ('Conditionalism') has a long history and very strong Biblical defense. For a selection of resources on the subject the reader can contact the author at comfaithnet@gmail.com. One can refer to pages 291-296 of Clyde E. Hewitt's Midnight and Morning (Venture Books. Charlotte, NC. 1983) for an extensive list of those who have historically upheld this position.

understand this word, think of an undesirable weed in a garden which is grasped firmly at the base and torn up, roots and all, so that there is no chance left that it could reappear.

We are told: "Fret not yourself because of evildoers, and be not envious of the wicked, for the evil man *has no future*; the lamp of the wicked *will be put out*." (Proverbs 24:19-20 my emphasis).

The wicked person "has no future". There is no hope for a coming reward for the wicked; there will be no happy ending to this life and they cannot expect any hope for life after life. Instead, they "will be put out". When you blow out a candle, what happens to the wick? Does it keep burning? Does it continue to give off light? No. It may glow for a brief moment, and then it smokes and goes cold. So it will be with the one who rejects God's Living Wisdom; they will be completely quenched (Hebrew *da'ak*).

Do not be misled into thinking that after the wicked are removed from the land they somehow linger in other places. The wicked will not linger. Proverbs is distinct in its language which clearly warns of this complete destruction of the wicked.

Again: "when the tempest passes, the wicked *is no more...*" (10:25 my emphasis). Here the word is *ayin* which essentially means 'to become nothing'. The word is similar to the question 'where?' as in 'where is it?' When the tempest of God's judgment passes, the wicked are gone, unable to be found because they no longer exist.

We read further: "...he who pursues evil *will die*" (11:19 my emphasis). Unless the context informs us otherwise, words are to be taken in their plain sense. The word *maveth* means 'to be dead' and there is nothing in this verse to indicate that it should not be understood literally. Death means an ending of life, a cessation of function. It does not mean 'translated to a different plane of reality where some life process continues'. The wicked completely lose the capacity for life.

God created man from the dust of the ground, and then animated that shell with the 'breath of life' (not an 'immortal soul'). Only when that breath entered man did he become "a living being" (Genesis 2:7), and only so long as this breath continues in man does he remain alive. When the breath of life leaves, man dies: "when You take away their breath, they die and return to the dust" (Psalm 104:29). When a human dies, the body returns to dust, "for dust you are and to dust you will return" (Genesis 3:19), the breath of life "returns to God who gave it" (Ecclesiastes 12:7).

God intended deathlessness for humanity if they obeyed His command not to eat from the tree of knowledge. Through disobedience they forfeited that right as God plainly warned: "for when you eat of it *you will surely die*" (Genesis 2:17 my emphasis).

Scripture teaches us that man's *only* hope for eternal life is dependent or conditioned *completely* upon his reception of God's provision of salvation through His Messiah, Jesus. God re-gifts deathlessness to man *only through* Jesus Christ.

This is the clear and decisive Word of God.

Sometimes it seems that the wicked will get away with evil and the immorality. Maybe some are led to believe the cliché 'if you can't beat 'em, join 'em'. Living Wisdom looks us in the eye and says, 'don't even think it!' Solomon says that "the wicked are *overthrown*" (12:7 my emphasis). The word *haphak* is used to describe something that is decisively defeated, such as the cities of Sodom & Gomorrah. Can anyone find Sodom or Gomorrah? No; they are utterly wiped out.

The Psalmist writes: "O [YAHWEH]...your enemies shall perish; all evildoers shall be scattered" (Psalm 92:9). There is no record of God taking prisoners. God's enemies cannot hope to win against Him. They will be completely defeated.

I have taken time to lay these matters out not for academic purposes or for theological debate certainly not to push an 'agenda', but because we *must* recognize that *God is not playing games*. His Truth is neither optional nor up for debate. Refusal to receive God's wisdom carries with it the severest consequence of an irreversible destruction. David and Solomon understood this and we need to consider seriously the language they used to express it and not allegorize or spiritualize it away.

The teaching of the Scripture, both Old and New Testament shows on one end of the spectrum a continuing existence for the faithful through the provision of God's life giving power, and on the other end, for those called the 'wicked', an eternal[98] and irreversible destruction in which they are deprived altogether of life and existence as God removes His life giving power[99].

*

Following the way of the Lord is not a matter of subjective choices based on what one might 'feel'. The Bible offers a more stark analysis: it's a matter of life and death. Willful, deliberate, persistent sin of which a person is unrepentant is a death trap. If it is true that the "fear of [YAHWEH] is the beginning of wisdom" (9:10), and yet "fools despise wisdom and discipline"(1:7) the consequence is that the fool will *die* for lack of judgment" (10:21 my emphasis).

These are difficult matters to think through because they force us to take an accounting of ourselves to ask where we might be allowing the cracks to widen. Be encouraged! The fact that you are willing to ask the question is, to my mind, evidence that the Holy Spirit is at work in you, leading you on the path of Living Wisdom.

Be Wise.

---

[98] The 'eternal' aspect of final punishment is not the duration but the effects.

[99] While differences of opinion may remain, we can all surely agree that in the end those who reject God's offer of Living Wisdom will not enjoy the blessings of His everlasting Kingdom.

Chapter 12

GOD'S PERFECT WISDOM

Is it even possible to find Living Wisdom? And if we do can we get it right? It is true we may never pursue wisdom perfectly, but God would not lay out principles for His people to follow if He did not intend for us to find some measure of success!

~*Walking the Path of Living Wisdom*

In Proverbs 3:1-12 God sets forth a pathway for discovering Living Wisdom. Through a set of 'challenge-commands' we are given a series of positive choices through which we are enabled to pursue a life well lived.

~The first challenge-command is to *remember*: "My son, do not forget my teaching" (3:1).

At the time I was sketching out these thoughts, my younger daughter was finishing up the first part of her sixth grade year. As she reached one section of her online math exam she broke down in tears. When I asked why she was crying she said, "Dad I don't remember how to do this type of problem, and if I don't remember then I never really learned it!" With a bit of encouragement, she was in fact able to recall the correct method and did exceptionally well overall.

This episode caused me to ask, 'if we don't remember our lessons, have we really learned them?' Living Wisdom must be meditated upon and thought over. It must become as natural to us as our heart beating or our lungs breathing.

The command "do not forget" is a call to root the knowledge of wisdom in his heart. As the Psalmist writes, "I have stored up your word in my heart, that I might not sin against you" (Psalm 119:11). When sin comes to call it is not going to remind us first to recall wisdom; in fact it will likely do all it can to ensure that we *do not* remember! The commitment to remember wisdom is a critical step to developing a wise life.

Proverbs 3:2 tells the reader that the teaching will add "length of days and years of life and peace". Is following the pathway of wisdom a magical formula for long life? If I choose wisely am I guaranteed to add years to my life and peace to those years? Not necessarily, but I am surely in a better position to have these blessings than if I choose to ignore the way of wisdom.

When God's wisdom is unknown, forgotten or ignored as the quaint tradition of a bygone era, people leave themselves open to destructive patterns of thought and behavior which threaten to shorten life and inhibit peace in their minds, families and communities. Living Wisdom shows us a way of temperance and self-control which increase the possibilities for longer, happier, balanced lives.

~The second challenge-command is to *practice unfailing love*: "Let not steadfast love and faithfulness forsake you; bind them around your neck; write them on the tablet of your heart" (3:3).

The word translated as 'steadfast love' (KJV 'lovingkindness') is a wonderful Hebrew word, *chesed* (pronounced from the back of the throat causing you to spit on those around you!). The Hebrew *chesed* appears to be approximately equivalent to the Greek *agape*; a special type of love which comes only from God and flows through God's people. It is mercy and compassion and an overwhelming love growing from a life that is built on faithfulness to God and His truth. Love and faithfulness are often connected and "express the ideal relationship between people or between God and people"[100].

---

[100] Reyburn, William D. and Fry, Euan McG. *A Handbook on Proverbs*. UBS Old Testament Handbook Series. 2000. United Bible Societies. New York. Electronic Database: Biblesoft Inc.

Obviously *chesed* cannot be literally hung around the neck, so we must consider the figurative image as expressing both something precious, kept close to us, as well as something *obvious*, able to be seen by others. These traits associated with 'steadfast love' are to have a special place and should be abundantly evident in the life of the one walking in wisdom. Likewise, the call to write these qualities on the 'tablet of the heart' should be understood metaphorically as forming the core of a person walking in wisdom's path; the very center of every thought, word and deed. The resulting blessing is that "...you will find favor and good success in the sight of God and man" (3:4).

One of my annual holiday traditions is the reading of Charles Dickens' classic *A Christmas Carol*. The name 'Scrooge' has become associated with the most miserable, miserly and disagreeable behaviors and Scrooge's reputation was, up until the end of the story, a poor one indeed[101]. He rejected kindness and love for his fellow men and as a consequence, failed to find "favor and good success" with man or, if I understand Dickens' perspective, with God.

To live unwisely is to live as Scrooge prior to his encounter with the 'ghosts'. To live wisely is to live as a man or woman of charity and kindness and

---

[101] I wonder if our common assessment of Scrooge has missed Dickens' point entirely. It seems to me that the name 'Scrooge' should be associated with one who finds redemption and has their life transformed for good.

honesty. Again, a good reputation is not guaranteed, but we will certainly never gain a good reputation through a life of cruelty and falsehood.

~The third challenge-command, to *trust*, is revealed in these well known and often quoted words: "Trust in [YAHWEH] with all your heart, and do not lean on your own understanding. In all your ways acknowledge him, and he will make straight your paths" (3:5-6)[102].

Whereas the first two challenges were a call from the 'teacher' to his 'pupil', now the focus shifts to the relationship of that pupil towards the Master Teacher.

To 'trust' the Lord here means to have confidence in Him. The Hebrew form of the word is the imperative; a command in the strictest sense. Solomon does not leave his son an out in this instance, nor should any follower of YAHWEH look for one. It is an unequivocal summons to submit to the Lord rather than to 'lean on' or 'support' ourselves.

In what areas of life does this apply? Solomon is clear: "in *all* your ways"; every thought, every deed, every word, every hope, every dream, every plan. There is no area of life that falls outside the

---

[102] Proverbs 3:5-6 are some of the more commonly known quoted verses in the entire Bible. It concerns me though that too often we encourage people to memorize verses but not contexts. Committing Scripture to memory is important, but memorizing isolated verses without knowing how the author intended them to be used or understood can lead to grave mistakes in application.

purview of God. Some may take this to the extreme, seeking the Lord's will for what cereal to choose for breakfast or what shirt to wear, but I suppose, if they are sincere to seek God's direction and do not become paralyzed by indecision or puffed up by a legalistic mindset, let them be free to seek. Perhaps we would be better off being a bit more literal; after all, the Word of God says *all* your ways.

As a general principle, when we acknowledge (*yada* -'to know') God in all our ways we will find the guidance we need to make the right choices by which He will "make straight your path". The straight path is representative of God's good ways, as expressed by David in Psalm 5:8: "Lead me, O [YAHWEH], in your righteousness…make your way straight before me." By contrast a way that is 'crooked' is recognized as evil: "But those who turn aside to their crooked ways [YAHWEH] will lead away with evildoers" (Psalm 125:5).

To have one's path made straight is to be brought into alignment with God's best. Note that God Himself makes our paths straight. Even as the redeemed people of God our tendencies lead us towards paths that are less than straight. We regress to "lean on [our] own understanding" and invariably make the wrong decisions. Whatever insight we may think we have of the world, ourselves, our situations or even of God, these are woefully inadequate to help us tackle life or attain wisdom. This is not to say that we have no ability whatsoever, but that we often have a tendency to esteem our own abilities far more than we should.

The wise person will pursue a path that sets aside confidence in their own ability to navigate life in favor of trust in YAHWEH. They will assess themselves and their comprehension of the world around them and then yield themselves to the Lord. In doing so, He will reveal His path. He does this through His Word, through others who are pursuing wisdom (elders, pastors or other spiritually mature brothers and sisters), and most importantly, through the Holy Spirit. All these are available to us if we give up what we perceive to be our rights and yield control to Him, confessing His sovereignty—total control—over our ways.

This third challenge most likely resonates with many of you. When we've tried to work in our own power and come to the 'end of our rope', in our marriages, our parenting, our spiritual growth, etc., we either get upset and complain to God, or we give up and cry out to God. What if we took the challenge of Solomon seriously? What if from the outset we set aside any hope of achieving success in our own power and let ourselves be led by the Lord? He is the all knowing God with power and ability far beyond what we can "ask or think" (Ephesians 3:20).

~The fourth challenge-command is *to be humble:* "Be not wise in your own eyes; fear [YAHWEH], and turn away from evil" (3:7).

Self attained and proclaimed 'wisdom' is of little use in God's Kingdom plan. Man's wisdom tends to justify his own sin and waywardness, too often rejects God in part or in full and is a recipe for disaster. Solomon again calls on his son to 'fear' YAHWEH and give Him all honor and reverence. Such a posture before the Lord should allow us to more readily reject sin and evil; not that sin loses its grip entirely, but that its grip is greatly weakened.

Such wise living can open the way to some wonderfully beneficial results: "It will be healing to your flesh and refreshment to your bones" (3:8). Similar to the above thoughts regarding verse 2, the results of wise living would seem to be a physical and emotional salve. Scientists tell us that within minutes after a person stops smoking, the body begins a remarkable process of healing and repair[103]. This shows us that wise choices are healthy, life giving choices which honor the Lord and set us on the path of who and what He intends for us to be.

~The fifth challenge-command is the challenge *to be generous:* "Honor [YAHWEH] with your wealth and with the firstfruits of all your produce; then your barns will be filled with plenty, and your vats will be bursting with wine" (3:9-10).

You will recall that I made more detailed comment on these verses in the chapter regarding

[103] Wolfson, Elijah. *What Happens When You Quit Smoking?* (date unknown). Healthline Networks Inc. Web. Accessed 5/7/2015.

wisdom in our finances. To summarize some of those key points: we are to give God the first and best as Abel brought the 'fat portions' of the flock; we are to give cheerfully; we are to give, trusting God to meet our own needs. God's generosity should flow through His people.

~The wrap up of this section offers the final challenge-command: *to receive* YAHWEH's *discipline*: "My son, do not despise [YAHWEH's] discipline or be weary of his reproof, for [YAHWEH] reproves him whom he loves, as a father the son in whom he delights" (3:11-12).

What follows, rather than a traditional blessing which we have come to expect for choosing the way of wisdom, is instead an explanation of why the wise person will heed God's corrective influence. And what a wonderful reason it is!

God's love is manifested in His discipline. This seems strange perhaps, as our perspective of discipline is generally negative; we do not like to be rebuked or corrected. There are some people who cannot or will not accept fault or responsibility for anything, even when it is clear that they are the 'guilty' party. When believers do this, they cheat themselves out of a great blessing— the opportunity to recognize and understand their place in the family of God.

The discipline of the Lord is designed to keep His children on the path of wisdom; to guide them into making the correct life choices which lead to stronger, healthier, happier, more mature followers. He does not do this for those outside His family. To reject God's correction is to show that one either does not care about being part of the family or does not know what it means to be a child of the heavenly Father.

When God's children begin to wander from the path of wisdom, our loving heavenly Father will send corrective influences into our lives and through these measures we are called to consider these challenge-commands: remembering His commandments (3:1); living in kindness and truth (3:2-3); trusting Him completely and committing our ways to Him (3:5-6); being humble and revering Him (3:7); being generous (3:9).

The one seeking Living Wisdom knows who they are before God. They recognize their need of God and their responsibilities to this loving Father and to others. They understand how this knowledge must direct a whole life pattern.

~Jesus Christ - God's Perfect Wisdom

Wisdom is not something that man developed over time; it is not of human origin. Living Wisdom is 'divine', existing eternally because it is part of God Himself; personified in the Living Christ, "the power of God and *the wisdom* of God" (1 Corinthians 1:24 my emphasis), "in whom are hidden all the treasures *of wisdom* and knowledge" (Colossians 2:3 my emphasis).

We notice some very strong comparisons

between the Living Wisdom of Proverbs 8 and Jesus Christ. Wisdom is spoken of as being with YAHWEH before any act of creation had occurred (8:24); Jesus is affirmed to be "in the beginning with God" (John 1:2). Proverbs pictures Wisdom as a craftsman, aiding God in fashioning the universe (8:30); Jesus is declared to have been the prime instrument of the act of creation (John 1:3; Colossians 1:16; Hebrews 1:2). Wisdom thrilled at the wonder of creation, particularly mankind, because of all created things only mankind can respond to Wisdom; Jesus rejoiced at those who had their eyes opened to see and receive Him (Luke 10:21-22).

It was prophesied of the coming Messiah: "the Spirit of [YAHWEH] shall rest upon him, the Spirit of wisdom and understanding, the Spirit of counsel and might, the Spirit of knowledge and the fear of [YAHWEH]" (Isaiah 11:2). We cannot miss the clear influences of Proverbs in this verse. The coming One would have wisdom, etc., because He would know reverence for God—the 'fear of the Lord'.

The brief account of Jesus' childhood is bookended by strikingly similar statements rooted in the teaching of Proverbs. Upon the return of the Holy Family from Egypt, Luke writes: "And the child grew and became strong, *filled with wisdom*. And the favor of God was upon him" (Luke 2:40 my emphasis). Then, after the events surrounding the twelve-year-old Jesus at Passover, Luke records: "And Jesus increased in wisdom and in stature and in favor with God and man" (Luke 2:52 my emphasis). By these statements we are to understand that from His earliest days, Jesus sought Living Wisdom.

His public ministry demonstrated perfect wisdom as he dealt with immature disciples, religious and political opponents, betrayers and deniers. Time and again the people "were astonished, and said, 'Where did this man get this wisdom and these mighty works?'" (Matthew 13:54). Every word, every act was done with Living Wisdom.

Jesus stated His purpose was to save sinners who could not save themselves. By His sacrifice, Jesus released us from the trap of our sin and set us on the way of a renewed relationship with God. This is the wisdom of God of which Paul writes in 1 Corinthians 1. At His resurrection and ascension, Jesus was enthroned as Lord of all, exalted for His obedience to God's Living Wisdom.

*

You will recall in the introduction to this book that I issued a warning regarding the use of the Scripture. I commented that Scripture is given by God for the benefit of *His people* not the world in general. An unbeliever can be led to salvation through the Word of God, but the principles of Scripture cannot be truly lived out by those who have not been transformed by a work of God's

Holy Spirit through the New Birth of faith in Jesus the Christ. Once a person has been born again through faith in Jesus, the Holy Spirit comes into that person to empower them to "walk in the way of righteousness" (8:20).

If to find wisdom is to find life, then *Christ Himself* is the object of the search. Before you can be wise, you must know Him Who is perfect Wisdom. He is the Tree of Life which stood at the center of ancient Eden and will stand at the center of future Eden when the Kingdom of God is established in its eternal fullness.

Be Wise.

Chapter 13

CONCLUDING THOUGHTS

A life well lived before the Lord is indeed possible—but only as we choose to *heed* Wisdom's words and *walk in* Wisdom's ways. Free will, as we mentioned earlier, allows us to either accept or reject Living Wisdom.

~*The Power of 'IF'*

The opening verses of Proverbs 2 are extremely important for us to understand the conditions by which Living Wisdom may be attained and our responsibility to heed wisdom's call.

> "My son, *if* you receive my words and treasure up my commandments with you, making your ear attentive to wisdom and

> inclining your heart to understanding; yes, *if* you call out for insight and raise your voice for understanding, *if* you seek it like silver and search for it as for hidden treasures..."(2:1-4 my emphasis)

There is a lot of power in that little word 'if'. We wrestle, don't we, trying to balance the sovereign rule and power of God with the free will of humans. Both are taught and affirmed in the Scripture; both should be accepted as valid in spite of the discomfort we feel at the issue remaining unresolved. Thoughtful Christians feel the tension between these two realities as we go through life and understand that the confusion comes from our limitations not God's revelation. Solomon recognizes God's sovereignty (see 16:9 & 19:21) and also, in this passage, affirms man's responsibility.

If his son heeds the words offered; *if* he 'treasures' his father's commands and makes a choice of the will to know and follow wisdom and truth; *if* he cries out, presumably to God, for discernment and understanding as Solomon had done (1 Kings 3); *if* he will count the pursuit of wisdom as the most worthy of all treasure hunts, straining every effort to find it; *if* he will *choose* to do these things "*then* you will understand the fear of [YAHWEH] and find the knowledge of God" (2:5 my emphasis). On these conditions, God will reveal Himself and His ways—His Living Wisdom.

Those who by this faith submit to the Lord have the confidence that in addition to His wisdom, they also have His ongoing care, guidance and protection as "He preserves the way of His godly ones" (2:8 NASU). Again, it is not that God's people will not at times feel exposed or lost, but that ultimately they are under His care and, like Job, can only be touched by evil at His express permission (i.e. Job 1:12).

As mentioned earlier, Proverbs is a primer for a king. For the king to rule well he must know the right paths and be able to recognize the false paths. He must know what makes a man righteous and what makes him foolish. He must know what to defend and what to fight against. The promise of wisdom is discernment to understand these things. *If* Solomon's son will choose to seek out YAHWEH's wisdom, *if* he will look to YAHWEH as the sole source of that wisdom, *if* he will, as YAHWEH's representative, look to the welfare of the righteous, "*then* you will understand righteousness and justice and equity, every good path" (2:9 my emphasis). If he chooses not to follow the Lord, he can have no hope of living or ruling well. And neither can we.

Such knowledge is a delight and "pleasant to [the] soul" (2:10). When we see wisdom at work, how it blesses and benefits others, how can we not be pleased? *God's ways work!* Why do we continually seek other means for healthy and balanced living when all people profit from wisdom? We have a promise: "discretion will watch over you, understanding will guard you"

(2:11, 12) from the 'agents' of evil (as described in 2:12-19). "So you will walk in the way of the good and keep to the paths of the righteous" (2:20).

God does not, and never will, force Himself upon any person. One question I have often been asked is why God allowed our first parents to sin; why He created them knowing that they would turn from Him. My answer: God desired a relationship of love with His human creature, but for love to be genuine it must be freely accepted and willingly reciprocated, which means it may also be freely and willfully rejected. Similar to His love, God will not force His wisdom upon us; nor does He grant wisdom to any who are in rebellion or opposition to Him. The Biblical record shows that as Solomon drifted from his commitment to YAHWEH later in life, his decisions became more 'foolish' and devoid of the wisdom that characterized his earlier days. Similarly, Rehoboam failed to take the 'if' to heart and lost over half of his kingdom.

Does not that little word 'if' still hold the same power? Do we not face the same choice to seek God's ways or turn away from them? And if we seek we should expect to find. Is this not what Jesus told us?

> "Ask, and it will be given to you; seek, and you will find; knock, and it will be opened to you. For everyone who asks receives, and the one who seeks finds, and to the one who knocks it will be opened."

(Matthew 7:7-8)

What will you choose?

~*Lifelong Learning*

The pursuit and discovery of Living Wisdom is a lifelong process. Recall again these words of Proverbs 1:5: "Let the wise hear and increase in learning, and the one who understands obtain guidance..."

No matter how much we think we know we are never so smart that we cannot learn more. Sad to say, there are many older folks who feel that their learning days are behind them, as if their age disqualifies them from learning. It is always a great personal joy in teaching these 'senior saints' to watch their eyes light up as the Lord impresses a new truth upon their heart. And when they realize they can in fact learn, they are hungry for more.

Then there are some who believe that what they already know is sufficient and nothing new anyone has to say can be of any value to them. This arrogantly rebellious refusal to learn infects old and young alike. To me, such an unteachable spirit is one of the most disagreeable traits a person can possess. You can often identify this spirit in people who make authoritative pronouncements which are factually incorrect; who 'speak above the level of their knowledge'; who show no real thoughtful engagement with the subject at hand. If you call them out, they become highly offended. The proverb is true: "A fool takes no pleasure in understanding, but only in expressing his opinion" (18:2).

My best teaching flows from my *study* and not from what I think I know. I never want to fall into the trap of 'coasting', but must constantly sharpen my heart and my mind through diligent examination and wrestling with the Scripture. A mature teacher can lead the 'simple' into maturity only as they themselves are led by the Holy Spirit and the wiser voices He puts into our lives.

Proverbs goes to lengths to show us the value of seeking out knowledge and wisdom and to warn us about the consequences of refusing to learn in humility.

When asked His perspective of the greatest commandment, Jesus answered as any observant Jewish man would: "…you shall love the Lord your God with all your heart and with all your soul and with all your mind and with all your strength" (Mark 12:30 quoting Deuteronomy 6:5). Jesus understood that our entire being must be engaged in the worship of God. Our mind and intellect is one of the facets of our being. We are to employ the intellect given to us by our Creator

Yet Proverbs 28:26 seems to contradict this: "Whoever trusts in his own mind is a fool, but he who walks in wisdom will be delivered." If we examine that verse more closely we recognize that Solomon is warning against putting our *trust* in our own intellectual power. The one who puts confidence in his own ability, devoid of recognition of the Lord is a fool, but this does not invalidate the mind itself or our use of it.

The writers of Proverbs "...possessed astonishing confidence in the power of the intellect. By living according to the accumulated insights of past generations"[104] a wise life was not only possible but expected. They never lost sight of "a benevolent creator whose providential care brought security to those who practiced 'fear of the Lord'."[105]

God has given us the ability to think, to reason, to evaluate the world around us and make conclusions. This process is the result of using our mind, of bringing it under the Lordship of the Spirit of God.

Personified wisdom speaks with these words: "I love those who love me, and those who seek me *diligently* find me" (8:17 my emphasis). Think about that word 'diligence'. In Hebrew the word *shachar* has an understanding of rising early in the morning in a commitment to finding what is looked for. David wrote: "O God, thou art my God; *early* will I seek thee: my soul thirsteth for thee, my flesh longeth for thee in a dry and thirsty land, where no water is" (Psalm 63:1 KJV my emphasis)

According to the heading, at the time this Psalm

---

[104] Crenshaw, J.L., 'The Sage in Proverbs' as quoted by Matthews & Benjamin, *Social World of Ancient Israel 1250-587BCE*. p143
[105] Ibid.

was composed David was in the wilderness of Judah. This could have been one of a number of occasions when David found himself away from 'civilization'. David wanted to be satisfied with the Lord but he was not content to sit idly; he pledged to seek God 'early' and 'earnestly'[106].

Solomon tried his hand at all manner of living. He reflected, "I turned my heart to know and to search out and to seek wisdom" (Ecclesiastes 7:25). Wisdom must be diligently sought with our whole person; we touch Him with our 'feelings' or emotions as well as our intellect and then communicate this to others by serving them in love. This is a lifelong process of learning

What of someone who refuses to commit to the learning of Living Wisdom? I count over forty proverbs which speak of the negative results of this choice. To summarize, Solomon warned his son that if he refused or ignored the teaching he would "stray from the words of knowledge" (19:27). Once on that wandering path leading away from knowledge, making correct decisions becomes increasingly difficult. The person joins the ranks of 'fools' who no longer care for Living Wisdom, but only for earthly gain (17:24). They become a stumbling block for others (10:17) and lead everyone into "poverty and disgrace" (13:18) and "ruin" (10:8).

Truly "an intelligent heart acquires knowledge,

---

[106] The King James translates *shachar* as 'early' while the ESV and NIV render it 'earnestly'.

and the ear of the wise seeks knowledge" (18:15). I pray that you never cease your pursuit of God's truth; that you never feel you have learned all there is to learn. If you would show yourself to be truly desiring of Living Wisdom, commit yourself to the reading and study of the Word of God. Consider the works of the great Christian thinkers of the past and present. Commit to challenging and stretching your mind. Never stop learning.

~Wisdom's Closing Argument

Proverbs 9:1-18 returns us to Lady Wisdom and Madame Folly as they issue their invitations. These 'women' compete for the same crowd and issue the same call: "Whoever is simple, let him turn in here!" (9:4, 16). The similarities end there.

Lady Wisdom is hospitable and practical; prudent and disciplined. Her house is firm; its seven pillars are cut from rock (9:1). The number seven has long been understood in the Bible as representing perfection; pillars hewn from rock clearly indicate stability. Wisdom's home will never fall or fail. Her table is set to openly receive many guests (9:2). The 'meat' and 'wine' she serves are the fruits of her labor; obtained honestly and carefully prepared. It is filling and satisfying. She sends messengers into the streets, inviting all to come and promising: "by me your days will be multiplied, and years will be added to your life" (9:11).

Madame Folly lounges in her doorway, seductive, unprincipled and deceitful. As nothing is said about the quality of her house perhaps we are to consider it an unstable shanty. While her invitation is 'open' she invites people to eat bread "in secret" and drink of "stolen water" (9:17). She is loud and obnoxious. Her promises end in disaster, for the fool who enters "does not know that the dead are there, that her guests are in the depths of Sheol" (9:18).

Trappers have an effective way to catch a raccoon. They bait a trap with a shiny object which the raccoon cannot resist. It reaches in a small hole, wraps its paw around the shiny thing...and is caught; the hole is not big enough for it to get its 'fist' out. If it would drop the trinket it would be free, but it can't bring itself to let go and is killed by the hunter.

Wisdom is not flashy or glitzy. It does not rely on a 'wow factor' and so people might overlook it. Folly is exciting, it sparkles and shines, and then it kills. If people would let go, they could be free, but they can't seem to get away. The allure of sin catches us all at some point as we listen to the voice of Madame Folly rather than the quiet and simple invitation of Lady Wisdom.

Wisdom offers meat and wine, while the best Folly can give is a cheap loaf of bread and some water. Wisdom's food is of substance which satisfies the eater; the food of Folly leaves the eater empty and unsatisfied. One is a balanced diet, the other junk food. How often do we go for the junk?

For the one attuned to the Scripture, there is a definite connection here to John 10, in which Jesus teaches about the sheep hearing the voice of the true Shepherd. Not all are going to follow Living Wisdom, just as not all are going to follow Jesus. It is a gift of God's grace for those who hear the voices and can discern Wisdom's call; those who know that "the fear of YAHWEH is the beginning of wisdom, and the knowledge of the Holy One is insight" (9:10).

Can you hear Lady Wisdom?

~The End of the Matter

We have spoken much in these pages of those who are 'fools' and reject the call of Living Wisdom to their own destruction. But it does not have to be this way. We are, each one of us, faced with the free will choice to follow wisdom. She is not hidden, but "raises her voice in the public square" (1:20) and calls out for all to hear (1:21).

For those who choose her way, what joy is discovered! There is such great blessing in knowing there is peace and safety for body, mind and spirit as we are led away from destructive influences. Wisdom is our companion and will never leave us; there to rescue us even in the darkest moments.

Wisdom desires to be found; longs to become part of God's people. Wisdom says, "I love those who love me, and those who seek me diligently find me" (8:17). YAHWEH, Wisdom's author, told Israel: "You will seek me and find me. When you seek me with all your heart, I will be found by you..." (Jeremiah 29:13-14). Jesus, Wisdom in the flesh, promised: "all that the Father gives me will come to me, and whoever comes to me I will never cast out" (John 6:37). We can never forget that the attainment of Living Wisdom begins and ends in our relationship of reverent faith to the Living Lord.

In Solomon's view nothing could be more important or of greater value than finding wisdom. We know that when given the opportunity to choose anything from God, he chose wisdom (1 Kings 3:5-15). We have seen how he declared wisdom to be of more value than precious metals or gems (3:14-15) and that no desire could compare to wisdom (3:15). He did not always exercise wisdom, but knew that all the gold and riches and power of the world meant nothing apart from Living Wisdom.

Do you desire life? Living Wisdom holds the secret of long and healthy life (3:16). Do you desire 'wealth' and 'prestige'? Living Wisdom is the path to spiritual riches and honor (3:16). Do you desire a quiet life? The ways of Living Wisdom are pleasant and peaceful (3:17). Do you desire 'life after life'? Living Wisdom is the path to the "tree of life" (3:18). Those who lay hold of Living Wisdom are blessed indeed.

I will state this one last time, so there will be no mistake or confusion: To be truly wise, one must know Jesus Christ, the epitome of Living Wisdom. If you have taken hold of the nail-scarred hands, His riches are passed to you as your eternal inheritance; His honor is given as your new birthright. You are highly favored to have been chosen by Him for His glory! The promises and blessings of wisdom are wonderful, but the greatest promise, the most desired blessing, is Christ Himself Who invites us to join Him in the eternal Kingdom He is preparing.

Be Wise.

AFTERWARD

I acknowledged at the outset that my purpose in writing this book was to lay out a pattern for ordered, principle based living that God's people may become stronger, healthier, more effective disciples of Jesus Christ. Now, at the end, I pray that you have found the beginnings of a framework for a life well lived, rooted in God's Living Wisdom.

There is never enough time or space to say all that one might wish and I recognize that there is much more to every topic I have addressed and topics which I did not address at all. I am indebted to those who helped me trim and shape these pages and wish well to those who would pick up where I have left off.

One thing I hope has not been conveyed or assumed in any way is that I have perfectly discovered Living Wisdom. God knows this is not so. I have by no means attained wisdom in its fullness, nor do I expect ever to reach that goal on this side of the Kingdom of God; but it remains a goal which I aspire to! As I have often remarked, 'we cannot be perfect, but that is no excuse not to try.' I write from the midst of the challenges where I suspect most of you are, wobbling and teetering in the struggle to find God's wisdom for living.

I am reminded how much I continue to need the Living Wisdom which comes from the hand of our

Lord and I am grateful that I have a Great High Priest, Who intercedes for me each minute and sustains me by the power of His Spirit. I know that as a child of the Living God, my Father desires me to live well before Him.

I hope that I have drawn closer to Living Wisdom in writing these pages to you, and pray you have received some measure of blessing from the Lord for reading them.

In closing, I would offer this prayer for you.

O Lord, in the Name of Jesus I pray that all those reading these words would choose to pursue Your Living Wisdom! I pray that they choose the reverence and honor of You, their God. Impart to them that knowledge and understanding by which they may live well before You. Let them never be counted among the fool, the simple or the mocker but among those who delight in You and are welcomed into Your gift of life 'in the land'. May they choose you O Lord in grateful recognition that You first chose them. May they offer You their praise and their lives in service to You, their Savior and King. Amen.

Be Wise!

Trinity, FL
December, 2015

RICHTER
PUBLISHING